Ecology, Environment,
and Education

THE PROFESSIONAL EDUCATION SERIES

Walter K. Beggs, *Editor*
Dean Emeritus
Teachers College
University of Nebraska

Royce H. Knapp, *Research Editor*
Regents Professor of Education
Teachers College
University of Nebraska

Ecology, Environment, and Education

by

R. THOMAS TANNER

Central Washington State College

PROFESSIONAL EDUCATORS PUBLICATIONS, INC.
LINCOLN, NEBRASKA

Library of Congress Catalog Card No.: 73-91543

ISBN   0-88224-073-0

Contents

Introduction

THE REEDS AT LETLHAKENG

The famous Scottish missionary, David Livingstone, explored southern and central Africa for over three decades, from 1841 until his death in 1873. He reached the Botletle River, in what is now the country of Botswana, in 1849. He wrote, "It is a glorious river.... The banks are extremely beautiful, lined with gigantic trees." Early explorers who followed him all described the Botletle as having swampy beds of reeds as well as forest along its margins, with populations of buffalo, elephant, and species of marsh-dwelling antelope. Immediately away from the river were open grasslands supporting giraffe, zebra, and various plains antelopes.

In 1851, exploring some 150 miles to the north of the Botletle, Livingstone crossed an open grassland of about 15 miles diameter. (Recently, an old man who first entered the area around 1900 confirmed that it had been a grassland then, with a few palm trees on the minor elevations protruding above the plain.)

Midway between this area and the Botletle is the Mababe River. Old people along the Mababe remember when wagons had to be floated across, while the oxen were unhitched and swam. That was back around the turn of the century.

Our first written descriptions of the Molopo and Nosob rivers, some four hundred miles to the south of the Botletle, also come to us from European explorers of the nineteenth century. Like the Botletle, they were lined with forest and swamps; the grassland away from the rivers contained springs favored by the wild animal populations. Even away from the springs, the people could suck water from the soil with a reed. The name of the village of Letlhakeng means "place of reeds," indicating a considerable amount of moisture in the area.

Today, Livingstone might find it difficult to recognize the places he visited. The forests and reed beds along the Botletle are gone, and the grassy plains back from the river have given way to bare ground, scattered bushes, and small thorn trees. The same is true of the grassy plain north of the Botletle. The Mababe, where wagons floated while oxen swam, is now perennially dry. The story is repeated along the Nosob and Molopo in the south. The rivers still contain some water, but the forests, swamps, and grasses have yielded to scrub bush. The springs are gone, and the people can no longer suck water from the soil with a reed. The large wild animals have either disappeared altogether or have been replaced by species that can browse on thorn trees and get by on little water.

And there are no more reeds at Letlhakeng.

Such changes have been carefully documented over all of what is today the nation of Botswana.[1] In just a little over a century, there has apparently been a marked deterioration toward desert conditions. Rainfall records have been kept for eighty years and indicate no downward trend, yet the area's water table has obviously made a significant drop, accompanied by pronounced changes in flora and fauna. What has caused the change?

Large numbers of people and their cattle migrated into the area in the 1800s, fleeing from tribal warfare elsewhere. In the last quarter of the century the warfare both within and outside the area was suppressed by the British, and the people were able to adopt a more settled way of life. As modern medicines were made available, a population explosion occurred among both people and cattle. Settled areas were overgrazed and a vicious cycle set in. Reduction of grass cover by grazing cattle exposed the soil, allowing more evaporation and faster runoff of water under the searing subtropical sun. This lowered the water table, thus making a less favorable habitat for grass, thus leading to more evaporation and runoff, and to the replacement of grass by scrub bush. In a large area along the Botletle, it appears that the process was caused by the setting up of a cattle-holding station by the Colonial Development Corporation in 1949. Up to ten thousand head were grazed in an area too fragile to accommodate them. In the grassy area which Livingstone found to the north of the Botletle, the cattle experienced a catastrophic die-off in the early 1950s, reducing a well-to-do village to poverty in three years. The entire country experienced severe drought in the mid-1960s. With soil no longer able to retain moisture, crops failed. Food had to be imported, and the people dug deep into dry river beds to obtain their water by the cupful. The cattle, which were the basis of the country's main industry, had to be disposed of; the single meat-processing plant was closed and has not reopened.

And there are no more reeds at Letlhakeng.

THE WAY IT IS

The earth as a life-support system is deteriorating. This the reader must understand clearly, in case he hasn't noticed or has been persuaded otherwise. In some respects our children's world will be better than ours, but on balance it will be uglier, less interesting, and more dangerous. This is not a pleasant fact to face, but denial is not a sufficient response to the problem.

Man has created deserts, and is still doing so, not just in Botswana, but elsewhere in Africa, in our own American West, and all around the globe.[2]

The world's human population increases by six million per month. That's one metropolitan Chicago. That's almost four Californias per year. The Population Council has calculated that if zero population growth is achieved in the developed world by 2000 and in the developing world by 2040 — an optimistic prediction — then the world's population will finally stabilize in about 2070 — *with over four times as many people as live on the earth today*. Yet today that rate of six million per month is accelerating, not slowing.

World energy consumption rose 63 percent during the period 1961 to 1970.[3]

Were all the people on earth today to enjoy the American standard of living, the annual drain on the earth's supply of finite mineral resources would be twelve times as much natural gas, one hundred times as much copper, six times as much petroleum, seventy-five times as much iron.[4]

Recent reports of the U.S. Geological Survey and the National Commission on Materials Policy warned that industrialized countries, particularly the United States, must reduce their consumption of certain seriously depleted resources, including asbestos, chromium, fluorine, mercury, silver, manganese, copper, gold, and iron. The commission recommended that no solution would be adequate without zero population growth.[5]

In 1800, the world's supply of cropland per person was four times as great as it is today. In 2000, it will be about one-half of what it is today.[6]

Since 1600, 359 species of animal life have become extinct. The rate accelerated in the last century, largely due to man's destruction of suitable habitat.[7] It is estimated that 100 species of mammals have become extinct in the last two thousand years, 75 of these having become extinct in the last two hundred. Thus the rate has accelerated from one species every 72 years to one every 2⅔ years.[8]

Bobcat pelts currently bring sixty dollars at the Seattle fur market, a situation which has stimulated heavy trapping of this useful predator. In the winter of 1972-73, twenty-five hundred eagles were caught in bobcat traps; over six hundred died.[9]

Six million acres in the United States have been destroyed by strip mining. That's two Connecticuts. The work goes on at the rate of 4,650 acres per week, or one more Connecticut per decade.[10]

Stream channelization—the straightening of streams for "flood control"—is a make-work process condemned by responsible ecologists and by even the most moderate environmentalists. It destroys all natural beauty along streams, eliminates fish and wildlife populations, and merely transfers flooding to other sites. The U.S. Soil Conservation Service has channelized twelve thousand miles of streams in this country. It plans to channelize ten thousand more miles—unless it is stopped in the courts.[11]

In Gary, Indiana, the death rate from lung disease is reportedly between two and four times the national average. One steel plant there emits eleven tons of soot and dust per hour, 40 percent of the total air pollution in the nation's worst area.[12]

About three-quarters of the American people live in the cities and suburbs of large metropolitan areas; about one-quarter live in rural areas, small towns, and isolated small cities. According to a 1969 Gallup Poll, they would be distributed in opposite proportions if they had the opportunity.[13]

Estimates of the amount of garbage produced annually by the average American range from one to twenty tons.[14]

That's the way it is.

A BLUEPRINT FOR SURVIVAL

Viewing such problems as if they were separate and unrelated leads to piecemeal, short-range solutions, which more often than not create more long-range environmental problems than they solve. An obvious example is the widespread use of DDT in the control of insect populations. DDT has contaminated waterways and endangered some species of wildlife.

The leading thinkers in the area of the environment have tried to point out the relatedness of many of our problems, and the necessity of sweeping, long-range solutions, which look not only tens of years, but also scores and hundreds of years, into the future. Some famous exponents of this approach are Paul Ehrlich, author of *The Population Bomb;* Barry Commoner, who has demonstrated the ways in which our current technologies are working against us; economist Kenneth Boulding, who has written of the basic economic changes necessary to accommodate the appropriate solutions.

A little book written in 1972 may be the best synthesis yet of what such people are saying. It brings environmental problems and their necessary solutions together into a single unified plan of action, literally a *Blueprint for Survival* (which happens to be the name of the book).

The authors of *Blueprint* first make it quite clear that there is a profound need for change, that the world's peoples cannot simply continue to drift along in a rather rudderless fashion as is now occurring.

They then proceed to their strategy for change on a global basis. The principal objective is that mankind be able to maintain itself indefinitely, in a system of dynamic equilibrium with the earth and her resources. If such an equilibrium were achieved, all the peoples of the world would be able to maintain themselves at reasonable levels of comfort and dignity, with useful employment available for all. There would be a varied and uncrowded world environment, with samples, at least, of all types of habitats and species, wild and domestic. Four main conditions would prevail: (1) minimum disruption of ecological processes; (2) maximum conservation of materials and energy—or an economy of stock rather than flow; (3) a human population whose numbers are stabilized at an optimum level; (4) social systems in which the individual can enjoy, rather than feel restricted by, the first three conditions. Let us examine each of these a little further.

Minimum Disruption of Ecological Processes

The use of "hard" pesticides—those that poison natural systems for a very long period of time before breaking down into simpler chemical compounds—will have to be discontinued immediately, in favor of "soft" pesticides. (This will be a very expensive step.) These, in turn, must be phased out in favor of an integrated pest-control program that uses natural predators, sterilization, and other means in favor of poisons, as much as this is possible. (Some poisons will always have to be used.)

Chemical fertilizers must be gradually but completely replaced by more traditional methods of soil husbandry: organic fertilizers such as manure (which is now discarded as waste, creating a pollution problem) and the rotation of different crops which variously use and renew different nutrients. (The growing use of chemical fertilizers on huge, single-crop farms leads not only to pollution but to eventual impoverishment of the soil. For soil to remain workable and retain moisture, it must have organic material such as manure and plant tissue decomposed back into it.)

Domestic sewage must be treated in such a way as to produce two end products: pure water and fertilizer. Industrial "wastes" must be recycled.

Conversion to an Economy of Stock

The industrial nations of the world now operate largely on an economy of flow: materials flow from their source (mines, farms, forests) to the consumer and quickly on to disposal sites in a one-way pattern of traffic. Since profits and incentives are directly related to the speed of this flow, people are valuable in large numbers as consumers (in that role they speed the flow) but are not valuable as workers (machines are faster). Thus modern industrial societies, as presently conceived, tend to increase unemployment on the one hand while needing people as consumers on the other, and they tend to use up and disperse both materials and energy (machines require more energy than workers) as rapidly as possible.

The conclusions seem almost obvious: a more preferable system would be one in which materials, as a capital stock, are retained through recycling, rather than treated as something to flow through the economic system and be depleted. Such a system would develop incentives to slow, rather than to speed, the flow. The implications of slow flow are several, and all fit together into a coherent economic whole. First, products will be made to last (in fast-flow economy, the aim is to make products having a short life). The manufacture of lasting products can employ large numbers of craftsmen who are not only gainfully employed but derive satisfaction from their work (worker satisfaction with assembly-line routine being a growing problem in modern manufacturing). The process of replacing some of our machines with people will mean that less energy will be required, so that "energy crises" will be less frequent. People will not be needed as consumers, thus removing an incentive for population growth.

Some measures are needed immediately: a raw materials tax proportional to the amount of raw materials used by an industry; an amortization tax inversely proportional to the life of the products produced (the tax would be high for short-lived products, low for long-lived ones); a power tax proportional to the amount of power used in manufacture. (Note that the flow economy-stock economy dimension is a separate issue from the communist-socialist-capitalist dimension. Countries must convert from flow to stock regardless of their stated politico-economic ideology.)

Stabilizing the Population

Although world population growth for another century seems inevitable, barring massive epidemics and starvation, population must eventually be stabilized at its optimum level. That will probably be a number equal to or considerably smaller than the present population of the earth. Once population *stability* is achieved, population *reduction* will be necessary. The means for this must, of course, be humane and preferably voluntary. It follows that massive education programs must be mounted at once, and sustained, everywhere.

By *optimum* population is meant that population level at which the peoples of the earth can live in harmony with the earth indefinitely, maintaining reasonable standards of health and well-being. The latter will include opportunities for satisfying employment and recreation, with a variety of natural and man-altered settings for both.

Creating a New Social System

In addition to the above, the crux of the new social system will be decentralization. Today, economic conditions force people of both the developed and less-developed countries to move to large cities. In the cities they are cut off from the agricultural-pastoral-natural environments that once gave employment and sustained the spirit; they are subjected to the social decay that is a well-documented statistic of all the world's urban centers, whether expressed in rising suicide rates, increased incidence of alcoholism, the spiraling number of violent crimes and accidents, or some other manifestation of deterioration.

A happier alternative—indeed, the only viable alternative—is a global pattern of small cities and towns, separated by countryside. For reasons that cannot be adequately summarized in so brief a space as this, such a pattern of population distribution would be more compatible with the measures suggested above, would be more satisfying and humane for the human inhabitants, would be more able to support diverse cultures, and would be more ecologically sound and attuned to the earth's resources than the present pattern of planless metropolitan growth, which is a global phenomenon.

Although the proposals stated above may seem radical to some, they are less so than might appear at first. The idea of small new cities away from the megalopolis has been propounded by many, including leading statesmen and politicians.[15] Government and foundations have supported research and planning on the idea, and such new cities as Reston, Virginia, are well beyond the mere drawing-board stage. Likewise, many American industries have engaged in recycling activities for years, and some industries are totally devoted to salvage and reuse of materials. Furturist groups such as Resources for the Future, which try to map out feasible alternative futures, are widely respected in government circles.

The *Blueprint* authors propose a series of actions which they feel the world's governments must undertake, beginning immediately. Their proposals are concrete and specific. Avoiding the pitfall of being pie-in-the-sky about what the world could be like two or three centuries hence, they clearly suggest how to get from here to there. They realize that the necessary steps will be disruptive, painful, supremely difficult. They know that progress as it has been popularly conceived until now is easy by comparison. Their thinking is, in brief, unabashedly utopian. There is increasing opinion, however, that utopian thinking is precisely what is needed if we are to avert disaster. By contrast, say the *Blueprint* authors, present policies of the world's governments are still primarily oriented to buying time and merely putting off the day of reckoning.[16]

SPACESHIP EARTH

Adlai Stevenson and Buckminster Fuller have been variously credited with coining the term "Spaceship Earth." The authors of *Blueprint* clearly understand the profound implications of the term:
In an expanding universe, the galaxies and stars grow farther apart each moment. The void of empty blackness through which they fly becomes ever larger, ever lonelier.

Our little Spaceship Earth whirls on through the fleeing stars of night. Except for sunlight, her fuel and supplies are all on board.

There's no going back for more,
And there's no getting off to go to some better place.
Spaceship Earth is off the pad,
And we're the crew.
The only crew she's got.

CHAPTER 1

Major Issues in Environmental Education

TWO SCHOOL PROGRAMS

Let us compare the environmental programs in two imaginary school districts.

In the Greenville School District, there is a concerted effort to introduce environmental studies at all grade levels and in all subjects, in ways that are appropriate to the subject areas and to the ages of the children. A full-time coordinator and staff have been hired to promote these efforts in environmental education (hereafter referred to as EE). Several workshops for teachers have been offered on the theory and practice of EE, with credit granted by a nearby university. A number of teachers have been given released time from their classes to prepare environment-related teaching materials. Special salary incentives are encouraging teachers to participate in the district-wide EE effort. New applicants for teaching positions are being screened on the basis of their knowledge of environmental topics and their commitment to introduce EE into their teaching.

As a result of all this, the environment is being studied in all subjects, at all grade levels, by most of the Greenville teachers and their students, and the numbers of both are increasing. Several of the kindergarten teachers take their children on nature walks, with the objective of instilling a "sense of wonder" in the children. In fact, they use Rachel Carson's little book *The Sense of Wonder* as their guide. Many of the primary and intermediate-grade teachers are using some of the contemporary EE curriculum materials to introduce environmental studies into all subject areas: mathematics, language arts, music, and so on. Some are using the *Earth Corps* program from *Scholastic* magazine, others the *People and Their Environment* books from the J. G. Ferguson Publishing Company, and still others are using various other materials. Most are adapting the materials, and picking and choosing from them, since they find them to be uneven in quality. At the junior high level, many classes are involved in investigations of community environmental problems. Some are checking the local streams, watching certain outflow pipes to see if any industries are discharging effluents at night, as is rumored to be the case. Others are doing a survey to see what different neighborhoods perceive to be the prime problems of the local environment. Others, as a part of their social science curriculum, are learning about the business world firsthand: they have begun a recycling corporation, have sold stock in it, and are selling bottles, cans, and paper back to industry for processing and reuse.

In the senior high schools a variety of activities is represented. Many of the teachers of modern foreign languages are using EE units developed by the Minnesota State Department of Education. Some of the home economics teachers have child day-care classes, in which their students staff day-care centers for preschool children; many of these teachers and high school students are engaging the children in sense-of-wonder walks on a one-to-one or one-to-two- or -three basis. Many physical education classes are learning lifetime sports activities that have a low environmental impact, such as archery. The relatively high impact of some sports, both as personal activities and as spectator sports, is discussed in these same classes: snowmobiling, waterskiing, auto racing, and others. Many English classes are reading poignant novels of the wild such as *Last of the Curlews* and *Year of the Whale*. And so on, throughout the entire school curriculum.

In the nearby suburb of Brownsville, the EE curriculum is quite different. A few teachers at all grade levels have taken the initiative to engage in activities similar to those at Greenville, but the only EE curriculum officially adopted by the school board consists of a one-week camping program for the sixth-graders each year. All sixth-grade teachers are required to participate, although they have received only minimal preparation for such an experience and some are not really interested. The district's "EE coordinator" is in fact a half-time teacher whose primary duties in "EE" consist of arranging the administrative details of the camping experience.

This experience consists of spending several days at a resident outdoor school site in the mountains two hundred miles from Brownsville. At camp, the children and their teachers engage in a variety of activities. There are field lessons on the topics of soils, water, plants, animals, compass, and wilderness survival. These tend to be unrelated to each other or to conservation concepts. They are required of all the children, who may also choose to attend additional sessions in archery, fishing, air riflery, or arts and crafts. The children have the experience of living in dorms, where they eat meals together family style and take turns at serving, cleaning up, and dishwashing. After meals and at evening campfire they sing songs which they have been learning all year, ranging from "On Top of Spaghetti" to "Bill Grogan's Goat." They also spend some time playing softball, baseball, and football; a few go on a nature hike with one teacher. At week's end, most agree they have had a good time, though several have been very homesick and one had to go home with a broken ankle suffered one night in some dormitory horseplay.

And, by week's end, the teachers agree that the children have profited by the week's program in "environmental education." The program's officially prescribed objectives seem to have been met: the children have learned "to live together in a give-and-take, living-and-learning situation." They have learned "how to survive in the woods" and use a compass. The teachers are convinced that many have "grown in maturity and responsibility."

Although the teachers seem confident that the program objectives have been met, and well they may have, an outside observer might wonder about the objectives themselves. Where, in this "EE program," are objectives such as "The children will understand our dependence upon this mountain environment as a source of clean water, lumber, inspiration, recreation, re-creation, and a variety of benefits," or "The children will be able to give examples of ways that these benefits conflict with one another as our population and our demands both grow"? Where is the objective that states, "The children will be able to express their own opinions logically as to whether population and demands *should* grow"? Where in this "EE program" are objectives such as "The children can demonstrate understanding of the finite, limited nature of our resources," or "The children will be able to describe the 'Spaceship Earth' idea"? Our outside observer, in fact, might conclude that there is a great vagueness if not confusion here regarding the goals and objectives of an "EE program."

ISSUE: THE PLACE OF EE IN THE SCHOOL CURRICULUM

EE may be treated as multidisciplinary—that is, it may be integrated into all subjects of the school curriculum. It may also be treated as a K-12 concern—that is, taught at any and all grade levels from kindergarten or first grade through grade 12. By contrast, it may be isolated in one subject or grade level. This is not really an issue among leaders in EE, since there seems to be universal agreement that EE should be K-12 and multidisciplinary.[1] It is much more an issue between the ideal and the real. There are many Brownsvilles. There are few if any Greenvilles.

Some state legislatures have mandated EE as a K-12 multidisciplinary concern, and a few school programs have been based upon this philosophy, with varying degrees of success. Most such programs known to us have been initiated by school districts, but only with considerable financial assistance from the federal government. This federal assistance takes the form of grants earmarked specifically for innovative programs in EE. In Green Bay, Wisconsin, Project I-C-E has involved teachers in writing some twelve hundred EE learning activities since 1970. These have been bound into booklets according to grade level and subject area, and distributed to other teachers, some of whom have received training in their use. Some 30-40 percent of the areas's seventy-five hundred teachers have used or adapted I-C-E materials. A somewhat similar program, in Mt.'Vernon, Washington, finds participating teachers preparing LAPS, or learning achievement packages. Each package is a self-contained, independent lesson meant to fit into the existing K-12 curriculum in various subject areas. The student obtains a LAP and proceeds through it at his own individual pace; he must pass a proficiency test on it before going on to the next. Some example LAPS include: "Animal Homes," apparently for primary grades; "Forest Trees of Washington," sixth grade; "Corporate Connivance," high school social sciences; "Housing and Land Use," grade level uncertain; "Populations," high school biology. The project staff tries to assure that each teacher develop a LAP of his own, and thoroughly understand the philosophy of the project, before trying LAPS prepared by other teachers.

The "K-12 Interdisciplinary EE Project" in Fort Lauderdale, Florida, prepares materials to be filtered into the existing curriculum, and trains teachers in their use. An emphasis of the program is on getting students actively involved in solving local environmental problems.

In 1970 and 1971, the EE project in Sedro Wooley, Washington, produced fourteen volumes of teacher-written and classroom-tested materials with such titles as: "An Environmental Approach to Art for Grades 7-9"; "A Save Our Trees Project for Primary Grades"; "An Environmentally Related Program for the First Grade"; "An Approach to EE: A Three-Stage Program for Intermediate Grades"; "Investigating Environmental Problems in a High School Biology Course"; "The

Project Physics Course (Modularized)"; "Developing Environmental Awareness in a Fifth-Grade Class of 'Below-Average' Achievement Level." This project was initiated and administered by Western Washington State College.

In 1971-72, in the high schools of Corvallis, Oregon, the Rachel Carson Project represented an attempt to introduce environmental studies into as many existing subject areas as possible. For instance, an American history class used Stewart Udall's book *The Quiet Crisis* as a supplemental textbook. This book focuses on the history of the relationship of the American people with the land, and traces the history of the American conservation movement. In an English class, some of the literature that was read included essays and poems from *Audubon* magazine, the satirical pollution poems of comedian Henry Gibson, and the beautiful, angry essays of Edward Abbey's book, *Desert Solitaire*. This class also viewed the Hollywood film version of the novel *The Roots of Heaven,* which is about a small army of idealists who wage war on elephant hunters in West Africa. A home economics class emphasized nonwasteful (and thus ecologically sound) homemaking practices. In a driver education class, students learned about Detroit's efforts in reducing pollution from autos, and also about the advantages and disadvantages of alternatives to the internal combustion engine, such as the steam car and the electric car.

Typing students found themselves typing script from various environmental publications. Thus, those who read as they typed were suddenly learning about conservation battles over this proposed dam or that proposed freeway. Physics students, after becoming familiar with the laws of thermodynamics, applied these to the problems of energy production in the future. They studied alternative forms of energy production, such as nuclear fission, nuclear fusion, the sun, and geothermal sources (hot water occurring naturally beneath the earth's surface). They regarded advantages and problems of each.

An assumption of this project was that the environment should be studied in each class *as appropriate to that class.* The integrity of each discipline was to be maintained: that which was studied in chemistry was clearly to be chemistry, or closely related to chemistry, and so on for other classes. This was in contrast to each teacher's simply conducting an occasional "mini-Earth Day," featuring some film cataloguing our environmental ills with seemingly endless minutes of crowded freeways and sudsy rivers. The latter approach would be *a*-disciplinary or *anti*-disciplinary rather than truly multidisciplinary.

It should not be supposed that all teachers in the Corvallis high schools participated in the Rachel Carson Project. As with the other projects mentioned above, its success was naturally limited by the number of teachers who were interested in participating. In a school or district of any size, this number never approaches 100 percent.

Why should EE be integrated into all subjects in the existing curriculum? Although many environmental educators assume that it should, they do not all explain the basis for the assumption. On the other hand, Noel McInnis, a leading environmental educator, feels that a root of our environmental dilemma lies in the fact that we have not learned to think ecologically. That is, we have learned to analyze, to "think the world to pieces," as McInnis puts it. But we have not learned to "think the world back together," to synthesize, to take a long-range whole-earth view. Thus we blithely dump pesticides onto the land to treat a single problem, with no mind to the multitude of other problems we create by so doing. We embrace economic growth for its desirable effects, while not heeding its undesirable ones. McInnis believes that dividing knowledge into disciplines, or subject areas, has contributed to this tunnel-vision mode of thinking. Thus, he concludes, "The present tendency to make environmental education another subject in the curriculum is merely adding to the fragmentation...."[2]

In his role as director of the Rachel Carson Project, this writer explained his reasons for integrating EE into the entire curriculum as follows:

The basic premise of the project is that a positive environmental ethic should pervade our culture, and that perhaps the best way to encourage this in the schools is to try to pervade the culture of the schools with this ethic or at least with its logical antecedents. The vehicle for this diffusion should be a subtle pervasion of the school, rather than an isolating of environmental studies in one or two new courses in "environment" or "ecology." The rationale for this can be set forth by example: "optimism," "industriousness," "pragmatism," and "materialism" are widely regarded as American traits. *We do not teach courses entitled "optimism" or "pragmatism."* If the internalizing of these values is, indeed, a part of the American enculturation experience, it is accomplished by more subtle and pervasive means. The Rachel Carson Project is, in part, an attempt to emulate these means. It was hoped that if teachers representing (nearly) all disciplines worked toward their normal course objectives, frequently utilizing environmental studies as their vehicles of instruction, it would subtly illustrate the desired and ideal—and yet unrealized—importance of the environment in our culture. As the project's associate director said one day to some art and English teachers, "You should develop the esthetic sensibilities of your students without ever mentioning that you are engaging in environmental education."[3]

In two separate articles in the *Journal of Environmental Education*, two other writers state a very similar rationale for their belief that EE should pervade the entire curriculum. Arnstein argues that we must undergo a change in values, accompanied by a "pervasive" examination of man's relationship to nature.[4] Studebaker states that EE can no longer be taught as "resource use education" in a single, science-oriented course, because EE must address "its controversial implications to our political, social, philosophical, religious and moral foundations. . . . EE should play a role more akin to that which patriotism or democracy now plays in the public school curriculum than to biology, chemistry, or any other subject. For like patriotism or democracy, respect for nature is a way of life."[5]

This necessity to establish an environmental ethic that will persist in a large segment of the population is certainly evident. One writer notes, "The new environmentalism could turn out to be only a passing fad, like hula-hoops. Americans are given to switching issues in midstream. Whatever happened to United Nations Day?"[6] With that writer, we remember with some dismay the completeness with which young America suddenly lost interest in the environment on the day that U.S. forces invaded Cambodia. It would seem that a more abiding concern is necessary, at least among a sizable fraction of the population.

Many environmental educators believe that such an abiding concern is most likely to result from EE that is integrated into the entire curriculum.

ISSUE: THE SCOPE AND DEFINITION OF EE

In the story of Brownville's "EE program," one might wonder what the compass and wilderness survival lessons have to do with environmental education. These *are* common elements of resident outdoor school (ROS) programs.[7] The children often enjoy them very much, especially the wilderness survival. But to what end are they taught? This is not always clear. If experiencing these lessons builds a rapport between child and wilderness, a positive feeling toward the out-of-doors and the world of nature, then perhaps these lessons are a healthy part of an EE program.

But when, as commonly occurs, children in an ROS construct "survival shelters" out of tree limbs and fallen branches, covering them with a thick roofing of living moss, which they have torn from the trees, and when the ROS site is literally covered by such devastation, one might validly ask whether this is an EE program or an anti-EE program.

The Brownsville children sing campfire songs, wash dishes, and learn to set table — do these activities really belong in an "EE program"? Perhaps. Perhaps the songs have a conservation theme. Perhaps the camp's kitchen personnel point out that the dishwasher relies only on very small amounts of detergent, explaining that this is a desirable circumstance environmentally. Perhaps they also point out that the dishes being set on the table do not include any plastic throwaways, despite the economy of certain pieces being of this nature. Perhaps. But not usually.

And how is one to evaluate a high school "EE program" that includes courses in "crime, housing, Africa, Afro-American history, Hispanic history?"[8]

What makes the course in Afro-American history part of an EE program? Is Afro-American history related to land-use practices? Or have the developers of the course simply chosen to label it as EE? What about the housing course? Is the need for housing related to the demand for lumber, and that in turn to our frantic cutting of the western forests, and that in turn to Senator Packwood's bill to limit log exports? Is it a housing course, or an *environmental* housing course?

A significant issue in EE, perhaps ultimately the most important issue, has to do with its scope. What concepts and methods are a part of EE? Which are not? Does EE have any boundaries that differentiate it from other educational efforts? If so, what are they? Or is EE anything and everything? Is it "all education," as has frequently been stated? How should EE be *defined*?

After reviewing a large number of EE programs and instructional materials from all over the country, a team of researchers at Ohio State University came to the following conclusion: "The reluctance of persons concerned with environmental problems and environmental education to define the area of their concerns has led to a diffuseness in the discussion of the problems which is unlikely to lead to useful analyses of the problems or to successful resolutions of them."[9]

A publication of the Social Science Education Consortium noted:

A very real education issue revolves around the definition of environment. At one extreme people are concerned about the "natural environment":

understanding natural processes well enough to deal with man's impact upon them, preserving examples of wilderness, optimum management of natural resources. At the other extreme people are concerned that children become sensitive to their total environment: observing everything around them, people as well as things, that they become responsive to the beauty and utility of the man-made as well as the natural surroundings.[10]

Other writers make similar observations. In reviewing a directory of current EE programs in elementary and secondary schools, one reviewer notes that the programs range "from 'classical' nature study to 'modern' urban studies. *Thus [is] reflected the fluidity of definition currently characterizing environmental education.*" (emphasis added).[11] Elsewhere we read that "the term environmental education is in itself most loosely defined."[12] Finally, states still another source, "A completely acceptable definition has not yet been found, for EE is a relatively new activity still undergoing important developments in its practical application and theoretical foundation."[13]

How, then, *should* one define EE? Or should one bother to do so? Some environmental educators see a definite need to make the effort. One wrote that in the program with which she was associated, "the word 'environment' has a very definite and significant meaning. This, in itself, is a refreshing change from the usual cliche-like tone the word has taken on, and unfortunately, *through its over-use and often mis-use, the word 'environment' has lost its serious impact*" (emphasis added).[14]

Likewise, argues another, "Lacking a single, uniform concept of the term 'conservation' and without a background in the principles that govern life, EE will fail as surely as conservation education has failed. Perhaps the first people who must be educated are the educators themselves."[15] He goes on to maintain that the progress of federally funded EE programs should not be overseen by a diverse, politically appointed committee which will fail to focus properly, but by a small committee of "eminently qualified ecologists and biologists." However satisfactory his proposal may or may not be, we share his concern.

This writer has argued in a professional journal that whereas EE may range across a diversity of topics and all subject-matter areas, it must not lose its central focus, which is the maintenance, for present and future generations, of a healthy, varied, and pleasant life-support system on the good Spaceship Earth.[16]

The reason for maintaining such a focus is simple: if we promiscuously attach the label *environmental education* to anything we are studying, merely because the label is currently in vogue, then that which is peculiar to EE and important about EE will be lost in a sea of insignificance and irrelevance. This fear is not groundless; it is based upon observation of a number of so-called EE programs in action today. We refer again to the high school "EE program" that contained courses in crime, housing, and so forth. Were the courses so focused in any degree? One cannot be sure. But we may rightly wonder as we read on, for the writer claims that this is "Environmental Studies in its [*sic*] broadest sense, which is openness, which is choice, which is individual work, which is people becoming independent and working with each other."[17]

We can only agree that this is indeed broad.

Another so-called EE program includes among its activities: "Make a wall of various textures," "Make a cardboard cutout of yourself," "Make a science-fiction movie."[18] We are not told the environmental-ecological significance of these activities.

Likewise, some typical activities from one very well-known EE program include the following: The students are to go out and find things they love and hate. They are to select a quality of themselves and record its changes. They are to list the stupidest things they do in school, analyze a popular song, speak only in the first person for a week, play the role of a perfect teacher, and so on.

The reasons that some teachers and other educators scurry off in all directions under the EE banner are many and varied. At least a few individuals are confused by the almost universally accepted call for "multidisciplinary" EE. Some interpret this to mean that because EE can be a part of every subject area, it follows that the study of anything and everything can properly be labeled as EE. The simple diagram will dispel this fallacy.

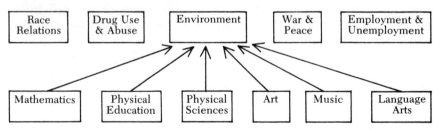

The top row of the diagram is a sample of human concerns with which the school curriculum might deal. The bottom row is a sample of the subject areas in the schools. Any of the problems at the top may be studied in a multidisciplinary fashion—that is, each problem may have a portion of each subject focused upon it, so that the school has a multidisciplinary program about racial relations, a multidisciplinary program about drugs, and so forth. Here we have diagramed a multidisciplinary EE program, with environmental studies receiving some attention from each subject matter. For instance, an elementary teacher may have the children create drawings (art) and writing (language arts) to express their feelings about their own community environs. They can then look for ecologically healthy and ecologically negative community characteristics in the writing and the drawings.

Some have argued that it is not proper to focus EE in the manner suggested by the diagram because the problems are all connected. This is quite true, and the study of the other problem areas may be a part of EE, *if* the connections are made. For instance, the study of unemployment *per se* is not EE. But if students examine the environmental effects of make-work projects (the proposed supersonic transport, certain highways and dams, certain wars), then the study of unemployment becomes EE. The study of drug abuse *per se* is not EE. But a useful analogy can be made between an individual whose system is dangerously dependent on drugs, and agricultural lands that have become addicted to large doses of chemical fertilizers, pesticides, herbicides, and other poisons. If a skillful teacher draws such an analogy out of his students, thus introducing a powerful EE lesson into the study of drug abuse, a "connection" will have been made.

Some persons concerned with environmental quality and EE may, in fact, be demonstrating a failure to make these very connections. Consider such statements as the following: "Despite the views of the overall environmentalists, it is more important to eliminate the Chicago slums than to clean up Lake Michigan," and "Just as important as it is to save our trees, it is more important to save our children [of the slums]"[19] Admittedly, these statements are here isolated from their original context, and they may have been meant to shock in the first place. Obviously, progress must be made on both fronts simultaneously. But any priorities which imply that we ought to forget our resource base and solve our other problems are shortsighted indeed. The simple truth is that other problems will only be compounded as resources are destroyed. Shortages of fresh water, open space, and energy sources will only encourage the growth of physical and social decay in man's communities, reducing all chances for recovery.

Another way of saying all this is to maintain that EE deals primarily with man-earth relationships. It deals with man-man relationships only as they affect, or are affected by, man-earth relationships.

The best thinking in EE has begun to clarify the distinction we have tried to make between *multidisciplinary* and *unfocused,* and has begun to "make the connections" between social problems that might not seem connected to someone who lacks an ecological perspective. For instance, a recent document from the U.S. Office of Environmental Education identifies *transportation* as an area which can be properly studied in an EE project, but quickly goes on to point out that "if some aspect of transportation is chosen as an area for an EE activity, the following kinds of questions would have to be examined, as appropriate to the activity: what are the impacts of present transportation modes on environmental pollution, land use planning, resource allocation, contributions to perception of crowding and actual crowding?"[20] In short, transportation is not a concern of the EE curriculum if we are asking only the relatively simple-minded questions: How many people can we move? How far? How fast? What is the cost (in dollars, only)? In these latter questions, there is a focus on transportation. In the questions quoted just before them, the focus is on *environment,* though the questions all have to do with transportation.

One enthusiastic reviewer of this particular document feels it accommodates so many different views of EE so well that it should limit future debate over the scope and definition of EE, if not actually putting such arguments to rest.[21] We would add that if the document accomplishes this, it is partly because of its author's ability to see the environmental-ecological connections between and among a variety of societal phenomena, such as transportation, human settlements, food production, and the impact of science and technology.

Likewise, Professor Clay Schoenfeld gives us a broad but well disciplined discussion of several characteristic aspects of EE. First, he says, EE deals with the environment of *man,* especially as his growing numbers place increasing pressures on that environment. Second, it concerns the *total* environment as affected by the interaction of man with the world in which he lives; it does not deal just with cities or just with nature, but with our attempts at coexistence of the two. Third, it is *interdisciplinary.* Fourth, it seeks *long-term solutions* to human problems — that is, ecologically sound solutions instead of short-term, simplistic ones, such as dumping nerve gas into the ocean in the hope of disposing of it. Finally, it should lead to *an integrated environmental ethic.*[22]

We are also impressed with the definition offered by Paul Yambert and Jerry Gafney of Southern Illinois University. They state that EE must deal forthrightly with three principles, which they state as follows:

1. Eventually no significant quantity of nonrenewable resources will be available.
2. Eventually humans will have to live in a steady-state ecology with a stable population and consumption based on a sustained-yield basis.
3. If the world is to be managed, it must be done so as a single ecosystem; piecemeal problem-solving and piecemeal resource management will fail.[23]

While one might question the word *ecology* as used here, these principles could certainly provide a focus for study and debate in an EE curriculum.

A similar function would be served by seven "propositions" found in still another definition of EE:

1. Although temporary solutions to specific environmental problems must necessarily continue to be found locally and regionally, a satisfactory solution of the complex of environmental problems can be found only with increasing international cooperation and planetary planning evolving possibly to a One World government. Such problems as the regulation of the ocean fisheries and international competition to produce an SST make this all too clear.
2. The United States should take the lead in establishing a humane, livable—yes, a *pleasant* planet, on which our posterity can live.
3. When this is achieved, the planet will necessarily have fewer human inhabitants than it does today, far fewer than it will have in the year 2000.
4. Such a planet will by definition be characterized by a more equitable distribution of resources than today's; there will no longer be "haves" and "have nots" among nations or regions.
5. All this *may* imply (though it may not, depending upon the safety of our technological breakthroughs in energy production) that eventually man's use of energy will again be limited by the rate at which earth receives energy from the sun, as was true before man began burning fossil fuels. At any rate, man should be intellectually and emotionally prepared for this eventuality.
6. In order to maximize human choice and freedom, the greatest possible variety of habitats, both natural and man-made, must be maintained. The implications for species preservation, habitat preservation, and human numbers are direct and clear.

7. Most, if not all, of man's encroachments upon the natural world at this time and in the future are by definition in violation of the above propositions. Such encroachments as are absolutely necessary must be initiated only with reluctance, with the informed and freely given consent of a wider constituency than those having an immediate economic interest in the encroachment, and with all due regard for posterity.[24]

This definition, prepared by the writer of this book while he was serving as a member of a national EE committee, maintained that the EE curriculum for high school students should include discussion and study of these propositions and of the facts and assumptions that underlie them. Students were to "examine, weigh, and discuss freely" the propositions. It further maintained that the EE curriculum for younger learners would consist of experiences prerequisite to the "intelligent discussion" of these propositions, although it did not suggest what these experiences might be.

Many prominent and knowledgeable environmental educators have apparently recognized the need to define EE. They have responded in the most direct possible way — by writing a definition. A colleague has compiled a number of these, all written in the last few years. Most are very brief; in fact, most who attempt a definition of EE seem to regard brevity as a major objective. Thus, these definitions tend to be generalizations with which no one can argue. Indeed, everyone will readily agree that students should gain "positive attitudes and values regarding the environment." A strength of these modern definitions is that they tend to update the venerable concept of "wise resource use," as we will see below in the section treating EE and conservation education. A weakness is that they tend not to offer specifics to shoot at and to argue with, as do the last two definitions.

The problem of definition is inseparable from the next issue, as we will see immediately.

ISSUE: CONTENT VERSUS METHODOLOGY IN EE

The problem of defining the scope of EE is compounded by the fact that some environmental educators tend to define EE in terms of its content, or subject matter, while others define it primarily in terms of its methods of teaching and learning. One writer refers to these two camps, respectively, as the "plain facts" people and the "process" people.[25] In preparing a government document for use by a wide spectrum of environmental educators, another writer found it necessary to include two rather detailed definitions of EE, one for each camp. These were entitled "Working Definition #1 (emphasizing process and theory)" and "Working Definition #2 (emphasizing content and purposes)."[26]

This book has already devoted some space to the content of EE. What are the views of those who define EE in terms of its methodologies?

They stress such procedural things as active involvement of learners — getting out into the community to gather pollution data, recycle bottles, do river cleanups, take political action, and the like. They emphasize open-ended investigation in which teachers and students learn together, in contrast to the teacher's being an authority who is expected to know all the answers and give all the information. They talk of a supportive classroom atmosphere in which students gain confidence in themselves by finding answers for themselves. The students have freedom to choose what they will study and how they will study it.

Process-oriented environmental educators usually contrast this kind of learning atmosphere with one in which the teacher confines himself to the textbook, expects students to gain irrelevant and outdated information, and generally creates a passive, dull, classroom atmosphere.

Some of those who define EE in terms of methodology are particularly sensitive to the child as a human being who must first feel reasonably good about himself if he is to care about his environment. A leading spokesman for this point of view is Noel McInnis, who has directed EE workshops around the country and who sits on the board of directors of the National Association for Environmental Education. In much of his writing, he has clearly demonstrated that he understands the content and purposes of EE. For instance, one of the teaching strategies he suggests is that the teacher challenge the students to devise a plan for "ecologically sabotaging the planet's life-support system." They will come up with massive releases of nuclear radiation, overuse of pesticides, or campaigns to encourage high human fertility. As they proceed, they may come to see remarkable similarities between their sabotage plans and things that are actually being done to earth right now.[27] It is obvious that McInnis fully understands, and is concerned about, the proper content and scope of EE. Yet in the bulk of his recent writing and speaking, he has gone beyond content to develop at length his belief that "what ultimately makes education environmental is not its subject matter, but its procedures." He recognizes that earth can only be helped by people who have the will, the self-esteem, and the experience to do so. Thus he questions schooling which for twelve years subjects the learner daily to an environment which "disregards his feelings . . . emphasizes his mistakes . . . assumes his ignorance . . . confines his body . . . confines his energy . . . confines his senses," and so on.[28]

The Environmental Studies Project in Boulder, Colorado, is likewise dedicated primarily to the methodology of EE and, like McInnis, it is most concerned with the feelings and self-perception of the learner. The project's focus upon the content of EE is minimal. The project's newsletter for Winter 1973 is a representative expression of project philosophy. Two of the eight pages are dedicated to an article entitled "Action Learning." This includes twenty-four examples of role-playing situations that a class might try. Only one of these is clearly ecological-environmental in its content: "Enact the saving of Lake Erie from destruction through pollution." Typical of the others are, "Defy gravity," "Create a mental hospital," "Create a general store." Another three-and-one-half pages are devoted to sociometry, the study of how children form groups according to their likes and dislikes of each other. There is a half-page on the "Spontaneity Theory of Learning." The final paragraph of this article suggests that spontaneous learning leads to the creative responses necessary for human welfare and survival. The newsletter contains no other references to the content and purposes of EE as discussed in this book. The seventh page is devoted to routine business matters, the eighth to a full-page poster, which captures the project's philosophy with the words, "Who Am I? I am my heritage . . . my values, and I am who I have the courage to be. Where Do I Fit? I fit wherever I have the capability and conviction to fit."

In summary, some environmental educators define EE primarily in terms of its teaching-learning methods. Some of these educators are especially concerned about the feelings and self-perceptions of the learners; all are concerned that the children become active participants in their own education.

To encourage a more active methodology in EE is certainly quite appropriate. We should note, however, that the idea is not new, nor was it invented by environmental educators, nor has it been promoted only by environmental educators. A half-century ago, the great American philosopher of education, John Dewey, was urging teachers to get students out of their seats and out of their classrooms, to learn their community firsthand, just as children are given to doing naturally when not constrained by school and parent.

Likewise, there was a wave of reform in science teaching around 1960, which produced many new textbooks and teaching materials based on the idea of "inquiry," meaning active investigation by the student, who was to find answers for himself. In this instance, however, the objects and tools of inquiry were more likely to be test tubes than townships, and the relevance of this curriculum reform has been questioned.[29] Also in the 1960s, a number of new programs in the teaching of English and the social studies were based on this general theory of teaching and learning.[30] More recently, many experimental schools have sprung up, dedicated to the ideas of open-endedness, inquiry, active involvement in the community, and the building of confidence in the learner, who is to see himself as one who can seek and find answers for himself. Most of these "alternative" schools are private, a few are public. A noteworthy example of the latter is the Parkway Project in Philadelphia, where high school students spend the bulk of their time at the post office, the factory, the river, the park, or wherever their investigations take them. Their progress is evaluated during occasional meetings with their teachers and fellow students, which are held irregularly and in a variety of places. The Metro program in Chicago is similar.

Thus, it would be naive indeed to think that the teaching methodology frequently ascribed to EE is either the invention or the exclusive domain of the environmental educator. It might be argued by some that John Dewey and the Parkway teachers *were (are)* environmental educators because of their methods, whether they so labeled themselves or not. Such a definition of the term *environmental educator* is certainly permissible; for our purposes here, however, we are regarding environmental educators as those who identify themselves as such, and who label what they do as EE.

Although the teaching-learning methods we have described are not peculiar to EE, they may be especially appropriate for it. This is because the condition of the environment has increasingly become a matter of popular rather than strictly professional concern. At one time, the populace at large tended to assume that the public agencies in charge of our natural resources were providing adequate guardianship, although a few small citizens' groups expressed concern to the contrary. In recent years volunteer conservation groups have grown, and citizens lobby, sue, and utilize other means to establish greater popular control over decisions having environmental impact. It follows that if the public is to take greater responsibility for controlling the institutions and practices meant to serve it, then the public should be educated in the practice of responsibility. It must be educated to take some active control of society's destiny, rather than passively witnessing the events that affect it and then passing into history.

It follows from this, in turn, that a methodology of teaching that places responsibility upon the student for his own learning, leading him actively to examine and try to influence the real world, may be a desirable procedure indeed. It must, however, give the student much more experience in the political process than has generally been the case to date.

In summary, environmental educators who emphasize the methodology of environmental education, and define EE in terms of its procedures, are quite right to do so. They are being consistent with what we know about how people learn, with evolving school reform in all subject areas, and with the recent history of the conservation movement as a whole. However, there is some danger that they will inadvertently mislead others into thinking that EE is defined only by its procedures. As we have seen, these procedures were advanced long before EE came into vogue. EE must be defined also in terms of its content—in terms of the body of knowledge, concepts, and ideas peculiar to it.

A balanced view of content versus methods is found in a document issued by the U.S. Office of Environmental Education:

> There are many . . . ways to impart and acquire the kinds of information, perspectives, and techniques that are essential in developing the environmental awareness and skills that our society needs. Many of these ways involve an emphasis on learner-directed and discovery-guided inquiry; some involve innovative and integrative learning outside the classroom. But in certain cases, environmental education must operate through more traditional approaches, such as lectures, classroom activities, and other nonexperience oriented educational methods if the learner is to attain some of the essential skills, concepts, and facts he needs.[31]

Those skills, concepts, and facts have to do, ultimately and primarily, with preserving the life-support system of our little spaceship.

Emphasis: Local-Immediate Versus Global-Futuristic

Many teachers involved with EE have their students learning about their local environments. Some have the students do research on local environmental problems, and the students of a very few may even go so far as to take political action to solve these problems. (To date, this last step appears to be promoted in writing a good deal more than it is practiced in actuality.) This approach is justified on the grounds that students are most interested in whatever is immediate, concrete, and real to them. Furthermore, Rachel Carson's "sense of wonder" is perhaps best developed in league with Alan Gussow's "sense of place." Gussow, an artist, has noted that people are more likely to identify with a *place* than with the more general concept of "environment," and that they become environmentally concerned when they observe undesirable changes occurring in that place over time.[32] This idea is given some support by the research of psychologists[33] and by autobiographical comments of dedicated environmentalists.[34]

Among those teachers who concentrate on local study, and on problems that are immediate both in time and space, probably many also try to develop in their students a viewpoint which looks at our environmental situation on a planetary, long-range basis. This is proper; eventually, students should gain a futuristic world view akin to that of *Blueprint for Survival*, realizing that the entire planet is a single ecosystem, and that equilibrium will take some time to achieve and will need to be a perpetual process thereafter.[35]

Inquiry Methods in EE

The idea of having the student learn by active inquiry into the world around him has long been among the least understood and most malpracticed concepts in education. Twenty years after John Dewey sold the idea to a large segment of the teaching profession, he was compelled to write a book gently scolding them for their prostitution of his ideas.[36]

More than a few of the outdoors-oriented programs are based upon a so-called inquiry approach. Examination of the methods and teaching lessons of these programs often reveals a format something like this: The teacher is facing thirty squirming students. He asks a long string of suggested questions. They dutifully guess at the answers, but they never learn what the answers are, for the teacher doesn't know, and no investigation will be made to determine them.

No one really cares, anyway, for the questions were rather boring in the first place. Throughout the grilling process, the teacher chooses one of two methods: (1) Asking each question of only one or two students, while the minds of the others exit the "inquiry" session. (2) Dragging an answer out of every student, while the minds of the others exit the "inquiry" session.

What makes this an "inquiry lesson"? Apparently it is so regarded simply because the teacher has not acted as an authority figure who tells the answers!

A superior concept of inquiry in EE finds students involved in community research and action programs like those described in Chapter 3.

A superior concept of inquiry in the out-of-doors finds students in a situation considerably less structured than the one described above, a situation designed to pique their curiosity (and perhaps their sense of wonder) by turning them loose in small groups for one or two hours:

1. With a variety of well-illustrated, easy-to-use identification books, with instructions to identify as many plants and animals as they can, without collecting, and/or
2. With a handful of unique rocks found in a stream, proceeding up the stream and its tributaries to see if they can find where the rocks came from, and/or
3. To find a place in the stream that was once an island, noting all the evidences they can that indicate it was an island, and/or
4. To answer the two questions, Do certain kinds of plants grow only in certain kinds of places? Do certain kinds of plants live with or near each other? Bring back only one leaf or twig from each kind as evidence, and/or
5. Similar investigations wherein they have opportunity to *find* some of the answers, and enjoy themselves doing so.

CHAPTER 2

More Issues in Environmental Education

ISSUE: URBAN EE

Many concerned educators feel that EE for the inner-city child must begin where the child is—that is, it must be relevant to his world and his experiences. Thus, they say, it cannot deal with white middle-class concerns such as wilderness preservation. Rather, it must begin with the problems of the child's immediate habitat: rats and cock-roaches, garbage-littered streets, crime, drugs, chronic unemployment. "How can you expect a child who doesn't have enough to eat to be concerned about the Great Auk?" asks one writer.[1] Another cites several reasons that inner-city blacks have been little interested in the environmental movement, pointing out that the symptoms of environmental deterioration have been more concentrated upon them than anyone: they have no access to the out-of-doors, their jobs tend to be the most pollution-prone.[2] States another, "An oil slick off the coast of California presents less of a threat in the eyes of a ghetto father than does a rat-infested garbage heap in which his children play. . . . City man must develop an understanding of his partnership with other city human beings and city institutions before he can appreciate or even seek to understand his role in the overall scheme of nature."[3] Finally, another writer argues, taking the city child out into the world of nature will not suffice, since he lacks the previous experience that would enable him to gain much of value from such ventures. "A sense of partnership with the world of nature and human beings that surrounds the city child may have to be established before he can feel a partnership with nature 'out there.'" Thus, he must study neighborhood planning, waste disposal, water supply, man's growth within the city, and how the city came to exist in the first place.[4]

A few educators have responded to the special needs of urban children by preparing "urban environmental investigations" along the lines suggested by the writers just cited. These are meant to help students and their teachers in exploring their neighborhoods; a sample of these materials is reviewed in Chapter 3. An insightful reader sympathetic to this approach will probably conclude that the materials available so far have just begun to scratch the surface.

Instructional materials are of no value, of course, without programs in which they are actively utilized. A few programs more or less exemplify the philosophy of urban education that we have been discussing. For instance, a junior high school program in a blighted area of Brooklyn involved its students in firsthand investigations and surveys of the local environment: "gutted buildings, broken fire hydrants, abandoned autos, garbage-strewn streets." It is reported that the students "participated in the political processes. . . . organized to improve community living."[5] The program was supported with federal funds. The National Audubon Society, with financial assistance from the City Garden Clubs, has trained several hundred New York City elementary teachers in methods of "urban ecology." Although the Audubon program uses the immediate environment of the urban school, it is primarily a nature-study program, utilizing investigations of such birds, plants, and insects as may be found in the area. The instructional materials that accompany this program are described in Chapter 3. Another training program for New York City elementary teachers is conducted by Fordham University and the Wave Hill Center for Environmental Studies. The project philosophy is apparently similar in some respects to that of the Audubon program, since the teachers "accompany the children on discovery trips to learn all they can about plants, trees, animals, etc.," apparently in the neighborhood of the school as well as at the Wave Hill Center.[6] Staff of the National Capital Parks in Washington, D.C., have in recent years brought a number of programs to the children of that city. Some of these are nature programs, others have to do with black history and culture, many are meant to familiarize children and young people with features in the area, such as the White House, the home of Frederick Douglass, and the Lincoln Memorial.[7] Other EE programs around the country include investigations of the urban environment. In the written descriptions of these programs, however, it is not always clear whether they are for the poor and disadvantaged children of the inner city or their more fortunate counterparts from the near-in suburbs. Something which *does* become clear is that initiative and money for programs often come from outside the schools, often from foundations and citizens' groups.

We have seen that some environmental educators believe inner-city children should study the "environments" in which they must live each day. Not all agree. Some say that society owes these children a direct contact with the natural world from which their lives are so divorced. Some programs have been based upon this philosophy. For instance, the National Audubon Society states that "tens of thousands of children who have never seen wild animals, swamps or forests are taken each year to our sanctuaries or to our Nature Centers."[8]

In 1969, under the auspices of another volunteer organization, black fourth- and fifth-graders from the ghetto areas of Washington, D.C., spent two weeks exploring the more or less natural environs of a forty-acre estate in suburban Chevy Chase. Since many had little previous experience with any but their own city environment, they were given the opportunity to explore, to use all their senses in experiencing grass, bark, leaves, moss. Scavenger hunts and other games were used to encourage contact with the world of nature. It is reported that many "had never felt grass beneath their feet. . . . the pond terrified them [at first]."[9]

During the previous winter and spring, a pilot group of children had spent one morning a week at the estate, where those who were to be their summer teachers worked with them on an experimental basis. These children, too, were at first fearful of the seminatural setting, but by late spring they were happily holding masses of frog eggs in their cupped hands, watching the tadpoles hatch.

The program was undertaken and financed by a citizens' organization, the Audubon Naturalist Society, whose members volunteered their time as teachers. During the next school year and the following summer, the program was dropped in favor of one in which children explored their own neighborhoods. It is important to note that this change was for financial and other reasons, rather than because of any defect in the Chevy Chase program.

The Wave Hill Center in the Bronx has spacious grounds with cultivated gardens and natural woodlands, greenhouses, and two old mansions overlooking the Hudson River. Not only does the center assist teachers in and around their own classrooms, as mentioned earlier, but it has programs for classes that visit its nature trails. Around the country, there are many other more or less natural areas maintained as study sites; many of these receive some use by inner-city schools having a large proportion of disadvantaged children. These facilities are discussed further in Chapter 3.

Such programs, in which urban children utilize natural areas, may be justified on a number of grounds.[10] One is the matter of providing positive experiences in different and more pleasant habitats. Another is the need for children to understand the dependence of the city upon other habitats, such as the agricultural lands, which provide food, and the wilderness and semiwilderness areas, which provide fresh water. A third reason, perhaps more subtle but equally important, was suggested by René Dubos, the environmental philosopher: "The greatest crime committed in American cities may not be murder, rape or robbery, but rather the wholesale and constant exposure of children to noise, ugliness and garbage in the street, thereby conditioning them to accept public squalor as the normal state of affairs."[11] The National Audubon Society implies the same by saying, "Nature must at least be seen by oncoming generations if they are to value their heritage."[12]

Although EE for the inner-city child has perhaps received more attention as a special topic within EE, the environmental education of the *suburban* child presents special problems which cannot be ignored. He, too, is separated from the many different habitats that support the metropolitan area. Though he is not so completely isolated from them as the inner-city child, his own experiences with natural, pastoral, and agricultural habitats are severely limited compared to former generations of the American public. For him, such experiences are confined to hurried weekend jaunts and crowded campgrounds, and are mediated by mobile homes and campers, trail bikes and outboard motor boats. As yet, we cannot say with certainty what effect all this has on his potential for becoming an adult who is deeply and intelligently concerned about the environment. However, we are inclined to agree with the environmental educator who wrote, "As more people become producers of services or deal with resources secondarily, fewer have the opportunity for meaningful contact with the land. A feeling of alienation, or lack of purpose may be the result. People must be reunited, must 'identify' with the natural environment if they are to recognize its inherent value."[13]

The issue of urban (and suburban) EE cannot be separated from the issue of sequence, as we will now see.

ISSUE: THE SEQUENCE OF EE ACTIVITIES IN THE CURRICULUM

This in fact may be another nonissue, not because writers in the field are unanimous in their opinions, but because they are not as yet addressing themselves to it very much. However, existing instructional materials seem to reflect great differences in philosophy about sequence. If and as the field develops, the matter of sequence will certainly have to become a major area of concern. Should little children study problems of the environment, such as pollution? Some instructional materials would have them do so—for instance, the *Focus on Pollution* series, for grades K-3, from Xerox Corporation. Or should they first have positive experiences with the natural world, to develop a love for it which will make the subsequent study of problems more significant to them? At least one activities book states this belief in its foreword.[14]

Teachers of almost any grade level claim that their students can study social problems and develop genuine concern over them. For small children this holds true especially if the problems are local and can be experienced directly, or at least can be seen to affect them directly: "They want to take *our* water to Arizona and California?" Regardless of the readiness of young children to respond to a study of problems, it seems reasonable to suppose that positive experiences which foster a deep respect or love for the natural world would be a reasonable part of their EE curriculum, if not the totality of it. Were such values developed in the citizenry, then decisions that affect the environment—such as whether to build a jetport here or a pipeline there—might be subjected to much greater scrutiny by a far wider segment of the public than they have been, even during the new popular concern of recent years.

In *The Sense of Wonder*, Rachel Carson describes what may be the ideal EE curriculum for the preschool child. She often took her small nephew on walks through the woods and along the beach, allowing him to explore at his leisure the wonderful world of fallen leaves and snowflakes, of toadstools and tidepools. Her few questions prompted him to experience these things with all his senses, to ask questions of his own, to develop a "sense of wonder" at the natural world. This sense, Miss Carson maintained, would and should stay with a person throughout his lifetime.

By contrast, we have observed second-graders seated around a table, inside a schoolroom, verbalizing with their teacher over the evils of water pollution, and have been brought to wonder, Would it not be better for these children to be down at the nearest creek under the wise guidance of an adult who has a sense of wonder, developing such a sense of their own? Should they not study water pollution later, when their love for the creek will cause them to be really concerned over its fate? Are not these tender childhood years a time for joyous, firsthand experience? Is not this teacher putting the cart before the horse?

We do not know the answers to these questions, though the weight of research in child development and in the psychology of human learning would seem to be on our side. Such studies — such as those by the eminent Swiss psychologist Jean Piaget — consistently demonstrate that young children need plenty of concrete, firsthand experience; abstractions are not possible without prior experience.

In the years ahead, we will have to face up seriously to the following questions related to sequence, trying to answer them with formal research and/or with trial-and-error while attempting various approaches to teaching:

What childhood experiences are necessary for a deep, abiding, and intelligent concern for the environment? We need studies of those who have consistently demonstrated such concern, to see what common elements can be found in their childhood experiences. For instance, do they predominantly have rural and small-town backgrounds, which allowed frequent experience with more or less woodsy habitats? (This does seem to be true of a considerable portion of the most committed persons known to this writer.)

Should this prove to be true, how can we provide comparable experiences for a generation of whom 80 percent will grow up in urban-suburban complexes? Will the typical one-week resident outdoor school program for intermediate-grade children even begin to be sufficient? Can additional and satisfactory experiences with nature be found closer to home and to the schoolyard, even if on the microscale of a vacant lot or the weed-grown edge of a playground? (Though even these settings are fast disappearing from the immediate habitat of most children.) Would satisfactory results be obtained through vicarious study of the natural world, utilizing films, projection slides, or other media?

Will group experiences in the out-of-doors be satisfactory or must the child experience a great measure of solitude in order to have sufficiently deep experience? (Such solitude also seems typical of the childhood of many of the most deeply committed known to this writer.) One EE curriculum project — Project NEED from the National Park Service — tries to provide a measure of solitude in its resident outdoor school program. NEED calls for each child to stake out his own "place" at the ROS site. For one hour a day, the children go to their own places and are quiet. It is reported that often they are bored at first, but by week's end they are observing many phenomena close around them — the bark of squirrel or the crawl of bug — and look forward to the quiet time at their places.

We need to know if teachers are following this suggestion. If not, why not? ("Too hard to supervise the kids. Liability.") If so, is it working? Does an hour a day for one week, with dozens of other children within shouting distance, even begin to do the job?

If we cannot provide sufficient out-of-doors experiences for the children of the metropolitan areas, what kind of curriculum *can* we develop for them? Can they profit from early experiences in which they grapple directly and concretely with local problems? What experiences might these be? Litter cleanup? Simple methods of monitoring air pollution? Can we make these lead to adult commitment? Can we make them lead to an intelligent overview of the planetary ecosystem? Of the dependence of the metropolis upon the fate of other environments? Of the dependence of other environments upon the whims of the voters in the metropolis?

These, then, are the questions to be asked and answered. At this point, it is interesting to recall for a moment the proposals by the authors of *Blueprint for Survival*. If the decentralization of cities were accomplished as they wish, one of the big problems just discussed would definitely be minimized. That is, no children would be so drastically divorced from the countryside as most are today. Opportunities to develop the "sense of wonder" would be relatively close at hand. Here, then, we have a classic chicken-and-egg problem. Decentralization will not occur until enough people want it—but will they first have to develop a sense of wonder in order to want decentralization?

The matter of sequence has been considered by some EE curriculum projects, at least in very broad strokes. Project NEED, for instance, is said to emphasize appreciation in the primary grades, uses and abuses of our resources in the intermediate grades, and "responsible action" at the high school level. Only the materials for grades 3 through 6 have been published as yet, so it is not possible to see how this philosophy has been converted into the actual teaching materials.

In their book of readings, Troost and Altman provide an excellent overview of the field of EE.[15] The issue of sequence particularly impresses itself upon the reader, for the book offers descriptions of many actual programs, and these raise questions of the type we have been asking in this section. Here, for instance, is a school art fair in which a kindergarten girl has entered a poster captioned, "Presents for all the people who have died from pollution." The school's newspaper, the *Ecology News*, contains poems on pollution by eleven- and twelve-year-olds. "Soon everything will die," writes Elaine. "It will kill you, you [sic] baby, and you will die maybe," according to Phillip. "It's killing every lad," if we are to believe Melody. "Pretty soon we will all just die," says Nancy.

In short, most of the Troost-Altman programs exemplify a problem approach for young children, and perhaps a rather superficial one at that. One cannot but wonder whether commitment of any depth is being fostered in these children, especially since they will soon enough find out that they are not going to "all just die." This brings us to the next issue.

ISSUE: POSITIVE VERSUS NEGATIVE APPROACHES IN EE

To study our environmental dilemma seriously is to expose oneself and one's students to a great deal of saddening, disheartening information. Matthew Brennan, one of America's most respected environmental educators, has noted that EE must necessarily be a painful experience. It cannot be all sweetness and light; any EE curriculum other than the most superficial will inevitably carry the student to a deep sense of loss and possibly anger at what is happening to our world.[16]

As Brennan and others in the field recognize, however, a steady diet of bad news is probably unhealthy fare for the young.[17] It might foster pessimism and negativism, causing the young to "turn off" and "drop out," thus becoming "a part of the problem rather than a part of the solution," as the current idiom expresses so well.

This point of view is expressed with particular eloquence in the teachers's manual of A Place to Live, a book of environmental investigations from the National Audubon Society:

> Reacting to the deterioration of the environment, however, is a grim approach—realistic and extremely important—but too somber to be the only motivation for setting up a program in natural science for young children. Their childhood is far too precious for us ever to lose sight of the "here and now" for them. Every child is entitled to feel the comfort and security of knowing that nature embodies ordered systems and is neither alien nor frightening. Every child has a birthright to know the inner glow derived from feeling at home with nature, from marveling at the continuity of life, from watching a living thing develop. Every child, city or country bred—should have an opportunity to experience the wonderment and find the satisfaction, stimulation and adventure that comes from knowing the natural world.
>
> It is knowledge of this sort that leads to an appreciation of nature and a desire to safeguard it.[18]

In the schools, one way to counter environmental bad news with environmental good news would be to allow children and young people to become actively involved with local environmental problems. They might gather data on the polluting discharges from an industry, carrying their information to the industry and to responsible government agencies, and, if necessary, to the public. They might then see improvement—good news—as a direct result of their own efforts. (There is a danger, of course, that they will not see improvement— bad news.) This kind of firsthand approach is suggested by many environmental educators and has been tried by some, with varying degrees of success.

Another way to counter bad news is the case-study approach. Citizens *can* alter the decisions that business and government make about the future of our environment. Students can study in depth some specific cases in which this has happened, such as the Miami jetport or the proposed Grand Canyon dams. Sometimes a citizens' group may cooperate with industry to achieve a mutually beneficial and desirable result. Let us examine one instance in some detail: In 1973 the Union-Camp Corporation, a forest products company, gave fifty thousand acres of wilderness to the Nature Conservancy, a volunteer citizens' conservation group. The Nature Conservancy, in turn, conveyed the property to the U.S. Fish and Wildlife Service for creation of a national wildlife refuge. The transfer documents contained restrictions that protect the character of the property, which is part of the Great Dismal Swamp in Virginia. Though the name may seem forbidding to some, the swamp is an area of natural beauty, rich in wildlife. The property, roughly fourteen miles long and five to six miles wide, is within easy driving distance of major American cities. In order to make the gift possible, the Nature Conservancy had the property appraised three times, calculated the tax benefits to Union-Camp of making such a donation, and made all the arrangements for future management by the Fish and Wildlife Service. When the Nature Conservancy was able to demonstrate to Union-Camp that the transaction would be economically feasible for its stockholders, and that future protection as a wilderness would be adequate, the transfers were effected.[19]

Unfortunately, such success stories are as yet too infrequent. Just as with community research and action programs, the case studies do not always have such a happy ending.

In Chapter 3 the reader will learn where he can find more information on specific case studies.

It was said earlier that this issue of positive and negative approaches is inseparable from the issue of sequence. Obviously, some community-action programs and case studies are too sophisticated for young children. A coordinated K-12 program might tend to emphasize positive, sense-of-wonder experiences early. A study of problems and their solutions would tend to prevail later, though the sense-of-wonder experiences would be found throughout the K-12 sequence.[20] Again, much trial-and-error, and formal research, will be needed before environmental educators (including classroom teachers) can be confident about the best approach to a K-12 sequence or the best mix of positive-negative experiences. Neither current trends nor past history makes us confident that such trial and research will occur as rapidly as is needed.

Any discussion of sense-of-wonder kinds of experiences with the world of nature necessarily leads to the next issue.

ISSUE: COGNITIVE VERSUS AFFECTED DOMAINS IN EE

Teachers and educators frequently categorize learning experiences into several *domains*. The affective domain deals with attitudes and values; the cognitive with facts, concepts, and knowledge; the psychomotor with physical skills. Many educators seem to display a preference for one domain over another, and trends in education reflect trends in society as a whole in this regard. Around 1960, society was concerned that the USSR was outstripping us scientifically and technologically, especially in the development of weapons. Hence a wave of curriculum projects in the schools emphasized the cognitive domain, especially in science and mathematics. A decade later, very different trends were clearly afoot in the country. We had entered the Age of Aquarius. *Hair* and *Jesus Christ Superstar* were hits on Broadway, and a youth counterculture had affected the mainstream of American life in everything from language to dress. There was a new concern for the affective domain, for the primacy of human feelings and emotions, as reflected in sensitivity sessions, encounter groups, and the popularity of a book entitled *I'm OK—You're OK*. It is not surprising, then, that many of the activities prepared in current EE programs should place great emphasis on the affective domain.

For instance, in one lesson of *Scholastic* magazine's *Earth Corps* program, the learner responds to such questions as the following: "Have you ever seen a waterfall like the one in this photo? What words would you use to describe it? . . . If you were given a free trip to any beautiful natural place on Earth, what kind of place would you choose? . . . Write a poem or jot down a few words about one of the small things you found on your walk. How is it beautiful?" Elsewhere the learner is directed to a photo of a housing tract, and the lesson explores the developer's probable reasons — economic — for creating a place that is described as dull for people and unsuitable "for other animals." In general, this program has a very appropriate EE focus, with a view of the positive and negative in the affective domain.

The NEED program from the National Park Service has the student listen to music describing two rivers: Ferde Grofé's *Mississippi Suite* and Bedřich Smetana's *The Moldau*. The scenes described in each part of the two works are explained, to assist the student in conjuring up a mental image as he listens. Through the NEED materials he encounters works of art by masters that depict various natural and man-made habitats.

As these two brief examples suggest, the cognitive and affective domains are not neatly separated from each other. While engaging in these activities, the learner is, hopefully, increasing his language skills or gaining information regarding certain composers, artists, and their works.

What is the proper mix of the cognitive and affective, the rigorous and the nonrigorous, the knowing and feeling components in EE? And how is the balance affected by the age and maturity of the learner: an emphasis on the affective for younger children, and on the cognitive for older? As might be expected, those responsible for EE are not in complete agreement on the matter. In the teacher's guide of one set of instructional materials, we find that the materials are "an attempt to serve the affective. . . . if the affective is served, the cognitive will follow."[21] In contrast, Dr. Robert Roth, a noted environmental educator from Ohio State University, speaks out in the clearest of language:

Before the land ethic attitudes can be built, it seems probable that the ideas will have to be formulated in the cognitive, or verbal, level. Emotionalism, or affectivity *per se*, will not do the job in the present state of the art. All of our past experience with failures in conservation education clearly indicate this. The only effective programs have been those that began in the knowledge area and then proceeded to blend with the emotional.[22]

Likewise, a guest editorial by John Hendee in the *Journal of Environmental Education* argued that we should be teaching facts and

concepts about the environment, rather than trying to change attitudes. An emphasis on attitudes before facts would encourage students
to polarize on issues, Hendee feels. When adult decision-makers so
polarize, they end by compromising on facts, a process likely to gen-
erate environmentally unsound decisions. Better that children gain
knowledge not only of ecological principles, but of specific issues, the
objective arguments on both sides of the issues, and the way in which
potential decisions are made on the basis of these arguments and other
factors. Then let the attitude — and behaviors — take care of themselves:
the teacher has discharged his responsibility at that point.[23]

In the opening issue of the same journal another environmental
educator emphasized the importance of attitudes, but she then went
on to propose that "if the child acquires particular broad environmental understandings (knowledge) he will develop a social con-
science (attitudes) that will affect his behavior (actions) toward the
total environment."[24]

The weight of the thinking we have located to date seems to lie
with the primacy of the cognitive domain, though our sample is admittedly small — by no means have a large number of environmental
educators yet expressed any opinions on this matter in the professional literature.

As was mentioned in connection with the discussion of sequence,
examination of the early experience of those who display a lasting and
intelligent commitment to environmental quality may give us valuable
clues. For instance, Roger Tory Peterson is America's best-known
student and defender of wild bird species. In a speech given in 1971,
Mr. Peterson said that his career was inspired by his seventh-grade
teacher, who started a Junior Audubon Club. Peterson went on to say
that the most sophisticated ecologists and environmentalists known
to him did not start as generalists. Like him, they began with a specific
interest, such as birds, flowers, or marine zoology. As their knowledge
of that area grew, and their interest in it became more intense, they
grew concerned over the fate of that which they were studying. This
led to a wider knowledge of other sciences, of politics, and of ecology,
human and otherwise.[25]

Until we know more, it seems prudent to attempt a judicious mix
of the cognitive and affective domains at all grade levels. Recently,
one of this writer's students prepared a field investigation for sixth-
graders in which they were to enter the forest for a session of
"listening, touching, looking, tasting, smelling." The experiences
were not taken beyond a sensory level; the objective was to deepen
awareness and appreciation. We urged him to retain the experiences

he had prescribed in the lesson, but to see if he could focus them on one, just one, concept. Eventually he produced what we felt *was* a judicious mix, a lesson in which the learner had the opportunity to learn something of the biological concept of community succession. At the same time, the learner was not weighed down with a burden of discrete facts to be memorized or complicated laboratory procedures to be executed. In short, there was maximum opportunity for the cognitive learning to be satisfying and enjoyable; it was supported, not interfered with, by the pleasure of experiencing the woods through the five senses. Similarly, another student developed a two-hour lesson on watersheds, in which the learners explore the grounds of the Cispus Environmental Center and meet many examples of watersheds, from as large as a creek's watershed to as small as a storm drain's watershed on the parking lot. This leisurely paced exploration of the grounds, giving considerable experience with *one* concept, appears to be a fair balance in which the cognitive is not so demanding as to conflict with the pleasurable sensory experiences of the hike: the singing of birds, the rustle of leaves. These, on the other hand, are not allowed to displace completely the formal objective of this lesson: the learning of a specified concept.

We conclude this section on the affective and the cognitive domains by pointing out that the affective domain has historically been a "touchier" subject with school people than the cognitive. While the curriculum guides prepared by school districts and state education departments frequently state that children should develop "positive attitudes and values" regarding this or that, they are rarely more specific about what those attitudes and values should be. This is because the schools serve a public that holds diverse views and values. The schools are not in a position to prescribe attitudes except in the most general terms, which are open to a variety of interpretations.

Not only are values and attitudes not specified, but there is a reluctance to use terms that convey a deep emotion, such as *love*. This is true also of most utterances by teachers and others who are involved with environmental education, though we do find a number of exceptions. For instance, some of the writers in the *Journal of Environmental Education* are willing to be less bland. One says we need *"love* – love in the general sense – love for your own existence on this most interesting and baffling of planets – love for people. . . . you must love nature."[26] The editor pleads that "fear will not be enough as a longterm motivating factor. We need love."[27] Another writer, in reviewing the works of five modern American nature writers, concludes that their common message to us as environmental educators is that man, if he is to save himself, "must develop a feeling of love, a sense of morality concerning his natural environment."[28] Finally, another states that "the very young should first be friends with and love and feel the natural world . . . ."[29]

Such a love comes through strongly, for instance, in the beautiful, angry writing of Edward Abbey in *Desert Solitaire*, which this writer has found to be a particular favorite among the teachers who take his workshops. It is also interesting to note that the culture and history of the American Indian have stirred considerable interest in recent years. One Indian trait that has received particular attention is his great love for the earth.

This, imply some environmental educators, is the spirit our children must catch if they are to be worthy stewards of their own future.

ISSUE: EE VERSUS CONSERVATION EDUCATION

Many in EE are saying either that EE has already replaced the older set of practices known collectively as conservation education (CE), that it is currently in the process of replacing them, or that it must replace them. The first issue of the *Journal of Environmental Education* was subtitled, "Defining Environmental Education." No fewer than nine of the articles therein were devoted at least in part to distinguishing the newer set of practices from the older ones. The very first article in that issue, written by the editor, summarized what various environmental educators claim are the differences between CE and EE.[30] He developed sixteen pairs of contrasting terms to differentiate the two. Some of these are explained below:

Compartmentalized (CE) versus Comprehensive (EE). CE focused on forests, or soil, or water, or whatever, one resource at a time, with limited regard for their interaction.

Local (CE) versus Global (EE). EE recognizes that environmental problems do not respect man-made boundaries between communities, states, or nations, nor can they be treated as if they do.

Rural (CE) versus Urban (EE). While continuing to recognize man's dependence on the land, EE also treats urban problems and solutions. For a population that is now largely urban, the emphasis can no longer be on contour plowing and the building of check dams.

Appended rationales (CE) versus Indigenous concern (EE). Conservation once had to be justified in the name of economic development, depression relief, or national defense. Today there is a growing climate supportive of conservation on its own merits.

Terrestrial (CE) versus Universal (EE). Water and air pollution have now joined soil erosion and deforestation as areas of concern.

Gospel of efficiency (CE) versus Quest for quality (EE). Utilitarian goals of maximum extraction and production have yielded somewhat to spiritual and esthetic goals.

Technical impetus (CE) versus Public involvement (EE). Conservation was formerly left in the hands of the expert, the professional who worked for government or industry. The environment has recently become a concern of millions.

Unilateral solutions (CE) versus Open-ended options (EE). Related to the Compartmentalized-Comprehensive dichotomy. Solutions aimed squarely at a problem of one resource often have undesirable side-effects on others; an ecological perspective is required of problem-solvers.

Business as usual (CE) versus Sense of urgency (EE). Today an environmental crisis is recognized by many; previously it was not.

Elementary education (CE) versus Adult education (EE). Because of the urgency of the situation, EE must reach all ages immediately—including those who can affect the political process now.

Biophysical sciences (CE) versus Social sciences (EE). The environmental dilemma requires social as well as technological answers.

The reader will notice that some of the dichotomies refer to the educational process *per se*, while others seem to refer to societal changes that are or should be reflected in education. To make these dichotomies more concrete, let us examine a set of classroom teaching materials that generally seem to represent CE according to these criteria. Rather than "setting up a straw man" or "beating a dead horse" by choosing a mediocre set of CE materials, we will examine a really excellent CE series—the set of seven booklets entitled *Man Improves His World,* written by George Shaftel and Helen Heffernan, and published by L. W. Singer in 1963. These booklets are representative of the best practice and materials in the conservation education of one, two, or three decades ago. They contain a wealth of truly fascinating information. They are well written—it is actually difficult to put down any of the booklets, once begun. In these respects, the series is superior to many of the EE materials put together in recent years. The material appears to be for junior or senior high school use.

The series title obviously implies no sense of urgency—quite the opposite, in fact. The seven booklets are entitled *The Fisheries Story, The Minerals Story, The Soil Story,* and so on for . . . *Water* . . . , . . . *Energy* . . . , . . . *Wildlife* . . . , and . . . *Forestry* . . . .

A major emphasis of each book is the technological means by which productivity has been and will be increased for each of the above resources. For instance, alternative energy sources are described, including possible dams across the Strait of Gibraltar and Bab el Mandeb, separating a sea from an ocean in each case! (The sea would evaporate to a lower level; then ocean water would be allowed through the dam to produce hydroelectric power!) Or, exotic fishes could be "farmed" in ponds or rice paddies. The increase in soil productivity due to chemical fertilizers and pesticides is discussed. It is explained in *The Mineral Story* that strip-mining for coal is more efficient and less wasteful of coal than deep-shaft mining, both of which processes are thoroughly explained and illustrated. New strains of trees, which will grow bigger and faster, are being developed to increase the future productivity of our forests.

In each booklet, reference to other resources is infrequent, although water quality is a persistent concern to the authors, who discuss it in most of the booklets, not just in the one on water. The fisheries booklet points out that fish add to soil fertility when raised in rice paddies, although the authors do not sharply contrast this example of good husbandry with other current practices illustrating bad husbandry. We learn in *The Soil Story* that Soil Conservation Districts are now called Soil and Water Conservation Districts. For the most part, however, each book focuses on maximizing the productivity of a specific resource with little reference to others.

Reference to ecological side-effects upon other resources is particularly stiking for its absence. *Water* discusses the Glen Canyon and Aswan dams with no mention of the undesirable effects predicted for them or produced by them. It is acknowledged that logging and recreation in the national forests will both experience great growth during the remainder of the century, but there is no mention of the conflict inherent in the growth of these activities, or of the potential effects of such growth upon other resources, such as water. Not found in these booklets are the questions raised in recent years regarding the side-effects of alternative forms of energy production, the importing of exotic species, the use of chemical fertilizers and pesticides, or strip-mining. Interestingly, we did not find the word *ecology* in the 752 pages of the series, though we may have overlooked it. Similarly, there are no discussions of such urban-suburban matters as mass transit, land-use planning, and inner-city decay. The authors display considerable concern throughout regarding water pollution, but air pollution does not figure in the booklets at all.

The authors are aware of the great demands that a burgeoning world population will make upon the resource base in the future. They describe measures being taken to increase food production in other countries as well as in the United States. They do not discuss population-control measures, however.

The general impression likely to be conveyed by these materials is that there were many conservation problems in the past, most of which have already been dealt with successfully (many specific examples are given). Similarly, there are many problems today, and they are being dealt with. The same will be true of future problems. In general, then, things are proceeding more or less satisfactorily.

The descriptions of successful rehabilitation programs going on here and there may lead the reader to suppose that these have been widely adopted wherever they are needed, which would be a mistaken impression indeed. The word *expert* is used frequently — experts are the persons who have solved and are solving our conservation problems.

In some cases the authors explore the causes of these problems. When man is the cause, it is usually due to ignorance, which seems to be accepted implicitly as an understandable and forgivable quality. Though avarice or other of the baser human traits may be hinted at as a cause ("Some industries have considered it cheaper to pay an occasional fine than to clean up . . ."), this is infrequent and is never discussed at any length.

If the reader will now look back at the pairs of terms describing CE and EE, he will understand more clearly the distinctions between the two approaches. *Man Improves His World* fulfills the descriptions of CE in most respects, although it clearly shares with contemporary EE a global-universal emphasis rather than maintaining the local-terrestrial emphasis typical of most CE. It must be reiterated here that the series is excellent, and that much of its information is relevant and of interest today. It is a high-quality example of late-vintage CE.

We should note also that the series reflects accurately the political climate in which it was conceived. We had scarcely entered the turbulent sixties when the series was being written. Growth was still unquestionably good to most Americans. Also, the shadow of McCarthyism was not yet far distant in the past. To question "progress," growth, utilitarian endeavors, or the making of money was still somewhat un-American and therefore rendered one subject to suspicion if not reprisal. That this climate contributed to shaping CE cannot be denied.

One significant difference between CE and EE, at least potentially, is suggested by the Technical impetus versus Public involvement dichotomy mentioned earlier. CE tended to instill faith in the expert, as we have seen. It told us that the professional conservationists of government, industry, and other institutions were taking care of the nation's conservation problems. To be sure, CE admitted, much damage had been done to our natural resources during the last century, prior to the establishment of such agencies and positions, but now these ills were being corrected. *Man Improves His World* illustrates this trait of CE. We learn there that the Tennessee Valley Authority, with its dams and related projects, had rehabilitated a despoiled land, and that the U.S. Forest Service was properly managing the forests under Operation Multiple Use. We find that international agreements made in 1935 were protecting whales, and that a number of other pacts were safeguarding various fisheries around the world. Eight federal agencies are named as being just a sample of those involved with wildlife protection—a list reassuring in its very length. We are told that Soil Conservation Districts had repaired the Dust Bowl and were continuing the good work nationwide. We find general statements to the effect that more must be done, but in general the tone tends not to be alarming. We find one specific instance of a federal agency jeopardizing a resource managed by another—but just one.

So said CE. EE cannot. As the media have responded to popular interest in the environment, as citizens' action groups have increased their memberships and their publications, new messages are being broadcast. We now find old friends condemned: the TVA for strip-mining and polluting the air, the Forest Service for allowing excessive logging on its lands, the Conservation Service for seemingly trying to convert every river into a ditch, the Bureau of Reclamation for apparently attempting to dam every river that the Army Corps of Engineers doesn't dam first, and the Bureau of Land Management for allowing cattlemen to overgraze the public lands into desert conditions. We now learn that those agreements in 1935 did not help the whales adequately. International tensions over oceanic fishing territories put the lie to what we were told about international agreements regarding fisheries.

The editor of the *Journal of Environmental Education* expressed this dilemma as follows:

. . . the veteran resource organizations are not particularly ecological in their orientations. On the contrary, they tend to espouse unilateral programs and cultivate special interest clientele. For example, the Soil Conservation Service supports the drainage of the same wetlands the Bureau of Sport Fisheries and Wildlife seeks to preserve, the Corps of Engineers would inundate a national park without batting an eye, the Forest Service has never been much of a custodian of wilderness, the Bureau of Outdoor Recreation already represents yesterday's patrician focus, and "the farm-subsidy program encourages the mis-use of toxic chemicals, one-crop farming that destroys ecological diversity, and mechanization that drives jobless rural laborers into packed cities.[31]

What will be the response of the newer EE? Will it continue to promote unquestioning faith in the experts? Will it react with excessive negativism, interpreting the role of the resource agencies to be one of total incompetence or flagrant violation of public trust? A more desirable possibility is that the current emphasis on the *methodology* of EE may encourage community research and action programs that will teach youngsters to be active citizens in a participatory democracy. Unfortunately, such programs as yet seem to be promoted more than they are practiced. Also unfortunately, many teachers, teacher educators, and even some methods-oriented environmental educators are as yet largely unaware of the matters treated in these last four paragraphs.

The resource agencies have long participated in CE by offering teacher workshops, preparing supplementary instructional materials, providing guest speakers and films, and by sitting on state advisory committees in CE. (In fact, this is surely one reason that CE has tended to convey the trust in the professional which we have cited.) In the Pacific Northwest alone, the U.S. Forest Service has conducted workshops for several thousand teachers in recent years. Now various of these agencies are attempting to establish programs and services in the newer EE. What will be their role and influence? Though we cannot predict with certainty, it *is* certain that some insightful environmental educators will scrutinize their efforts.[32]

A final point. One must look beyond labels to decide whether a program — or a person — represents the newer EE or the older CE. Some "EE" programs seem to be CE programs relabeled. Conversely, some persons having a sound, intelligent understanding of EE proudly retain the title of "conservation educator." Examples include Dr. Matthew Brennan of the Brentree Environmental Center in Pennsylvania and Dr. Wilson Clark of Eastern Montana College.

CHAPTER 3

Selected Programs and Instructional Materials

PROGRAMS IN ACTION

Programs in School Districts

The six programs described in this section have several traits in common: They were all initiated by local or regional school districts, which applied for and received federal funding to make the projects possible. Most — but not all — were tentatively funded from 1971 through 1974, with annual renewal dependent upon performance. They generally represent a good command of the scope and methods of EE, and appear to range from good to excellent in their materials, methods, and/or achievements. Because of their recency, they have not yet received widespread attention. Finally, they represent a variety of interesting devices for getting EE into action, and for getting around the lack of interest inevitably demonstrated by some teachers and administrators.

In the EE Project of Topeka, Kansas, the project staff and teachers have developed, tested, and revised a number of instructional units for various subjects and grade levels. Units contain detailed lesson plans, background information, test items and discussion questions, objectives, and supplementary readings. Many of the units utilize the Topeka area to a greater or lesser degree. For instance, there is a geology unit centered on Calhoun Bluffs and the geological history of the area, and there is a unit on "Tire Production and Pollution Control," which utilizes the resources of the local Goodyear plant. There is a good balance of concepts, problems, and (potential) solutions in this unit and others. Though some of the topics are far-ranging, most are ultimately related to the central concerns of EE. For instance, some archery lessons at first glance appear to be a rehash of a standard item in the traditional outdoor school curriculum. Looking further, we

55

find that archery is advanced as a lifetime recreation having relatively low environmental impact (as compared, say, to the riding of trail bikes). This idea should have received even greater emphasis. On balance, these appear to be good materials.

The Topeka project offers workshops for interested teachers and helps them develop lessons and units for their own classes, over and above the units just described. In its first two years the project served one-third of the children in the city's public schools; it was anticipated that two-thirds would be reached by the end of the third year. Contact EE Project, Topeka Public Schools, 1601 Van Buren, Topeka, Kansas, 66612.

The program in Milwaukee, Wisconsin, has a variety of interesting components. One of the most unusual and exciting is the mini-proposal program, which encourages any elementary or high school student to initiate a proposal and submit it to the program for possible funding. Approved projects have had budgets ranging from forty-four dollars to six thousand dollars, and have included such titles as "Air Pollution Monitoring Station," "Humanities as an Aid to EE," "Determination of Asbestos Levels in the Air Supply in the Community Adjacent to South Division," and a "Film Festival" and "Ecology Operetta."

The program's urban field-trip program is also unique. Teams of teachers have developed and tested field-trip "packages" consisting of filmstrips, tapes, teacher's guides, and kits of classroom materials. These materials help teachers to take their students on field trips in Milwaukee. Classes prepare for the trips with pretrip lessons and follow up on them with continued classroom activities.

The program also sponsors workshops for teachers and students, and programs for emotionally and mentally handicapped children. It maintains a demonstration farm, and supports teams of teachers who write detailed instructional materials for various subject areas. Units prepared as of the summer of 1973 included home economics, junior high mathematics, chemistry, and English language arts; ten more units were completed by the fall.

Throughout almost all of these materials and activities, an appropriate focus for an EE program is maintained. During its first year, the program reached more than one-fourth of the children in the public schools. This appears to be an excellent program. Contact EE Coordinator, Milwaukee Public Schools, 5225 West Vliet Street, Milwaukee, Wisconsin, 53201.

In Milwaukee, students can propose a project. In Shawnee Mission, Kansas, teachers do so. All teachers in that city are eligible to prepare instructional units, or "modules," for a K-12 multidisciplinary curriculum in which EE is incorporated into existing classes. Project funds support the authors of successful proposals as they prepare modules, which include overview, objectives, lesson plans, tests, a list of supportive audiovisual materials, and references to resource persons and useful literature. A module is revised after testing in two classrooms other than the author's. In its first two years, the project produced ninety-five modules. These are available free to the public and parochial schools of the city, and may be purchased by others. Contact Project CLEAN, Shawnee Mission Public Schools, 9803 Rosehill Road, Shawnee Mission, Kansas 66204.

An unusual program was supported by federal funds in Atlanta from 1971 to 1973; the program continued with local funding in 1973-74. Interested high school students can take one or more quarters of independent study on individually chosen problems. During this period they take not more than two regular classes, and they can check out of the school as needed to pursue their research. Some of the problems chosen include: temperature inversions and their effect on air pollution, bacterial pollution of the Chattahoochee River, urbanization as related to violent crime in Atlanta, and the man-land relationship on a nearby Indian reservation. One talented girl is producing paintings, drawings, and photos (which she is taking, enlarging, and printing herself), and is writing essays, poetry, and a short play. Project staff circulate among the participating high schools to assist the students and their advisors, and also publish an excellent weekly newsletter. Contact EE Project, Atlanta Public Schools, 2875 Northside Drive, N.W., Atlanta, Georgia, 30305.

Project ECOS serves northern Westchester County and Putnam County in New York. It has initiated and supported a number of school-community activities. For instance, a county planner offered a special high school course in land-use planning. In another special course, students documented their town's need for a wetlands ordinance. In all nineteen school districts of the area, students are learning to monitor water quality—a favored activity in many action-oriented EE programs around the country. One fifth-grade teacher employs a year-long theme, "Peekskill: the re-making of a city." There is a weekly field trip, accompanied by a naturalist, illustrating the theme. ECOS has stimulated recycling projects at a number of schools, and these are turning a profit. Contact ECOS, Building 6, 845 Fox Meadow Road, Yorktown Heights, New York, 10598.

The EE Center in Portland, Oregon, is a cooperative project of the Portland Public Schools and Portland State University, though the support of many other agencies and individual volunteers has been received. It is funded by grants from the U.S. Office of Environmental Education and other agencies. Its functions are several: a self-learning center, with a collection of EE materials; a clearinghouse, where those with specific questions can be referred to each other or to appropriate organizations or agencies; a stimulator and coordinator of other EE efforts in the Portland area. Contact EE Center, 373 Lincoln Hall, Portland State University, Portland, Oregon, 97207.

Other EE Programs

The following programs also appear to range from good to excellent. They differ from the foregoing in that they are not school district operations, though most of them do work closely with school districts.

The Institute for Environmental Education, a private nonprofit group in Cleveland, conducts workshops in which teams of teachers and their students, working as equal partners, learn to investigate local environmental problems, and learn ways to move toward solving them. These teachers and students then continue their investigations at their own schools, and they are recruited by IEE to serve as workshop staff for teachers and students from other schools. IEE attempts to reach many schools in a given watershed area, and to coordinate their efforts in trying to solve the problems associated with that watershed. Workshops have been conducted in Tennessee, Wisconsin, Pennsylvania, and elsewhere. The best-known watershed project emerging from the workshops is the Cuyahoga project. Cleveland's Cuyahoga River gained fame a few years ago when it was so badly polluted that it caught fire—twice. Now, eight public schools, two private schools, and a parochial school are cooperating to study the river and to contribute to solving its problems. There is a highly regarded four-volume set of teaching materials associated with this program; it is entitled *A Curriculum Activities Guide to Environmental Studies*. For information, contact IEE, 8911 Euclid Avenue, Cleveland, Ohio, 44106.

Under the auspices of the Population Curriculum Study at the University of Delaware, teachers have developed three hundred "teaching packets," K-12 multidisciplinary, which are available to other teachers in the region. Revision and addition are ongoing. Six concepts are central; two have received the most work so far: "The activities of human populations may lead to conditions restricting the quality of life," and "By planning within the natural system, a life of acceptable quality can be provided for all people." Contact PCS at College of Education, University of Delaware, Newark, Delaware, 19711.

A program of potential interest to environmental educators is the new Environmental Alert Network of the Smithsonian Institution. In 1968, the Smithsonian established its Center for Short-Lived Phenomena, which receives and distributes reports regarding such phenomena as volcanic eruptions in Ethiopia, an increase in the lynx population of Minnesota, an oil spill off the coast of Maine, and a mouse plague in Australia. Today, twenty-three thousand scientists and agencies participate in the program. The Alert Network was officially initiated by the center in January 1973 to involve high school and college students. By June 1973, some forty-three thousand students in 660 high schools were participating, along with four thousand students in 98 colleges and universities. In that six-month period, the network was responsible for 39 percent (sixty-one) of the reports submitted to the center, and 23 percent (nineteen) of those which the center in turn reported to the international scientific community. The center has so far provided participating classes with an average of one event-report per day, and teachers have made various instructional uses of these. Feedback from students indicates that they are more interested in ecological events than events of other classes, and the center expects to initiate programs which involve students in the measurement of pollutants. Contact Smithsonian Institution, Office of Environmental Sciences, 60 Garden Street, Cambridge, Massachusetts, 02138.

The Chesapeake Bay Foundation is a citizens' group dedicated to a more orderly development of the bay, including preservation of invaluable estuaries and marshes. The foundation has for several years taken high school and college students on overnight cruises to study estuarine ecology, and it has produced an *Ecology Cruise Guide* for student use. Author-naturalist Euell Gibbons has accompanied some cruises, to lead the students in foraging for meals. The foundation has cooperated with public and private schools in serving between three hundred and five hundred students per year. CBF is also planning an environmental study center. Contact CBF, Box 1709, Annapolis, Maryland, 21404.

Outdoor Programs

The discussion of the Greenville and Brownsville programs in Chapter 1 may have left the impression that outdoor programs are unnecessary to EE. Quite to the contrary, well-handled outdoor programs are probably more necessary than ever, given a population in which the daily lives of four persons in every five are geographically isolated from the great out-of-doors. Description of some example programs and facilities is in order.

The Nolde Forest EE Center is a unique program. Supported by a federal grant from 1971 to 1974, it is located in the 644-acre Nolde Forest State Park in Pennsylvania. Its staff of teachers develop out-of-doors lessons and use these to instruct teachers and their students at the park. The unique feature here is that the staff also works with teachers to develop entire units of instruction, lasting perhaps six weeks, for use back in the classroom. The lessons at the center are, for these classes, an integral part of the units. (We must note, however, that some of the lessons reveal an inadequate concept of the inquiry process.) Unlike a number of outdoor programs, Nolde is dedicated to a K-12 multidisciplinary curriculum that appears to be genuinely ecological-environmental in its focus; the staff has obviously worked hard to develop and promote such a curriculum. The address: Box 392, R.D. 1, New Holland Road, Reading, Pennsylvania, 19607.

The Washoe Pines Ranch near Carson City, Nevada, provides an experience that public school programs might do well to emulate, within the practical restrictions imposed by their large size and modest budgets. The ranch conducts a five-week summer program for thirty children, aged eleven to fourteen. The youngsters take field excursions to the varied habitats of the area: dunes and marshes, pine forests and sagebrush desert, Pyramid Lake and Lassen Peak—and Reno. The exciting feature of the program, however, is the very appropriate spirit of the activites, which are meant to instill a strong identification between the learners and the land. They read literature about each area while exploring it; this includes the journals of early explorers and the essays of more recent writers. They engage in art projects using native materials, which they have learned to identify. They learn aspects of traditional and modern culture from the Paiute people of the area. They care for, and harvest from, the ranch garden.

It should be noted that the ranch actively recruits minority children to be a part of the groups, and finances their stay with scholarships. The entire life-style of the ranch, under the leadership of Dick and Maya Miller, lends a special quality to its various activities, such as an expedition over the Lewis and Clark route for fifteen- to eighteen-year-olds, and stimulating seminars for adults. Address: 6205 Franktown Road, Carson City, Nevada, 89701.

Glen Helen Nature Preserve in Ohio consists of one thousand acres, of which one-third are undisturbed forest and the remainder old farmland in various stages of succession toward a natural state. Glen Helen's Outdoor Education Center maintains a staff of eight teacher-naturalists who conduct lessons with the sixth-grade classes visiting the preserve each week. The teacher-naturalists are college graduates who receive training, room, board, college credit, and a modest salary during their five months of service. Inservice workshops for teachers, and a preservice student-teaching program out of the University of Dayton, are also conducted at Glen Helen. Address: Director, Glen Helen Outdoor Education Center, Antioch College, Yellow Springs, Ohio, 45387.

By way of contrast, the teachers whose classes visit the Cispus Environmental Center in Washington do their own teaching. However, a variety of workshops is offered at Cispus to assist those interested; one workshop is described in some detail in Chapter 4. The center buildings and facilities constitute an outstanding physical plant, beautifully and remotely situated in the Cascade Mountains. Cispus has a comprehensive collection of instructional materials in EE. It is operated by the Office of the State Superintendent for Public Instruction, and is utilized by school districts and other organizations for a variety of programs throughout the year. The most typical program is a one-week residence experience for intermediate-grade children. Address: Cispus Environmental Center, Randle, Washington, 98377.

The Balarat Center for Environmental Education is maintained by the Denver Public Schools. Located in the Rocky Mountains fifty miles from the city, the center is a 750-acre site with another 1,400 acres available for use by the thousands of Denver children who visit the site with their teachers on one-day field trips. Facilities are being developed which will allow the schools to have overnight ("residential") programs at Balarat. Eight of the Balarat staff members are high school students who work full time and receive full academic credit. Address: Director of Environmental Education, Denver Public Schools, 1521 Irving Street, Denver, Colorado, 80204.

The Woodfern Environmental Center is located on forty-five acres of rolling, wooded terrain on the shores of Lake Hartwell, South Carolina. Study areas include: wildlife management and forest management sites; science, weather, and air pollution stations; a colonial studies area, an arboretum and a garden, a listening area, and a nature trail for the blind. The staff attempts to develop K-12 multidisciplinary activities. Address: Anderson Public Schools, P.O. Drawer 439, Anderson, South Carolina, 29621.

A residence program operated by the Kenai Peninsula Borough School District in Soldotna, Alaska, finds sixth-graders staying in tents on one portion of the Kenai National Moose Range.

The National Audubon Society has been a pioneer in establishing nature centers in metropolitan areas, for the use of school children and others. Since 1961 it has maintained a Nature Centers Division, which has assisted in the planning of 180 such centers, usually by drawing up detailed plans for communities, colleges, and school districts. The society maintains five nature centers of its own, in Greenwich and Sharon, Connecticut, El Monte, California, Dayton, Ohio, and the newest—the Schlitz-Audubon Center, located nine miles north of Milwaukee on 185 acres along Lake Michigan. It might be added that the society sponsors two-week summer sessions in natural history for teachers and other adults, in outdoor settings in Wisconsin, Maine, Wyoming, and Connecticut.

Other outdoor facilities and programs are described in *EE/Facility Resources*, published by Educational Facilities Laboratories, 477 Madison Avenue, New York, New York, 10022. Examination of the projects it describes may cause the sensitive reader to wonder if some inadvertent—and undesirable—lessons will not be taught by a few of these facilities. For instance, at one site there is an underground observation center where students can watch a beaver family in its "natural" habitat. Will such a facility help build a sense of wonder? Or will it merely reinforce the tendency to view the natural world as something to be seen superficially, as by tourists—in a category with wax museums and Disneyland?

INSTRUCTIONAL MATERIALS

Case Studies

Much in our culture gives the impression that one is doing his duty as a citizen if he merely votes. A sound knowledge of environmental studies makes it clear that this concept is insufficient. The deterioration of our environment would proceed even faster were it not for citizens who voluntarily give of their time and money to influence the laws and practices that determine our future. This is the true essence of American participatory democracy, and the schools have a responsibility to teach it. A few EE programs attempt to give direct experience in responsible citizen action. This process of participatory democracy can also be studied vicariously through the use of case studies of specific environmental "battles." This is a plea for more published materials of this nature, since little now exists. One example is:

Survival Kit: Ecology and Social Action. Evanston, Ill.: Harper & Row, 1971. Teacher's and student manuals, brief eco-readers on various topics, film strips, records, posters. High school social science. Features a multimedia presentation of a battle involving pollution control at a General Motors plant in Tarrytown, New York. Includes recorded interviews with principals and towns-people; presents both sides fairly. Eco-readers include studies of Egypt's Aswan Dam and the supersonic transport. These materials are unusually candid; offending government agencies and individuals do not go unnamed. Entire thrust is on showing what citizens can do. A few of the discussion questions could be misleading; otherwise, an excellent set of materials.

Two other multimedia instructional packages might qualify as case studies of conservation battles if supplemented by other readings. They are:

Ecology at Work: The Case of the Bighorn Sheep. Pleasantville, N.Y.: Warren Schloat Productions (Prentice-Hall), 1971. Filmstrips, recorded narration, and teacher's guide. High school. Excellent. Researcher Jim Morgan finds that wild sheep are declining in numbers due to overgrazing of their range by domestic cattle. The filmstrips and tape alone comprise a fascinating and excellent study in wildlife research methods for a biology class. But the teacher should share pages 23-25 of the teacher's guide with the students, at which point this case starts to become an invaluable social studies lesson. In *Life* magazine for May 22, 1970, learn what happened to Morgan when he began whipping up public support on behalf of the sheep. Also see his articles, "Last Stand for the Bighorn," *National Geographic* (September 1973), and "The Nibbling Away of the West," *Reader's Digest* (December 1972). This combination of materials provides an excellent basis for a case study.

Man, Alaska, and Energy. Bellevue, Wash.: Alyeska Pipeline Service Company (P.O. Box 576), 1972. Filmstrips, recorded narration, reading materials. High school. Story of the Alaska oil pipeline, from the company which will build it. Alyeska is to be commended for addressing these materials directly to the environmental-ecological impact of the pipeline, rather than skirting these issues with irrelevant, straw-man, and *non-sequitur* arguments, as are often found in prodevelopment literature. Nevertheless, this material does not become a case study unless supplemented by magazine articles that give opposing arguments and detail the pipeline battle. (See below.)

While case-study materials designed for classroom use are few and far between, a wealth of information on current environmental "battles" can be found in the magazines published by certain voluntary citizens' organizations. Some of the best of these publications are:

Audubon, published six times per year by the National Audubon Society, 950 Third Avenue, New York, N.Y., 10022. Also contains beautiful photos and nature writing.

Conservation News and *Conservation Report,* published frequently by the National Wildlife Federation, 1412 Sixteenth Street, N.W., Washington, D.C., 20036. A free service supported by contributions.

The Living Wilderness, published quarterly by the Wilderness Society, 729 Fifteenth Street, N.W., Washington, D.C., 20005.

Students may also follow issues of a more local nature in publications from citizen groups closer to home, such as the periodical *Earthwatch Oregon,* from the Oregon Environmental Council.

Two groups of case studies for use in junior and senior high schools are currently being prepared with financial assistance from the U.S. Office of Environmental Education. This work is being done by the School of Public and Environmental Affairs, Indiana University, Box F, Bloomington, Indiana, 47401, and by the Conservation Foundation, 1717 Massachusetts Avenue, N.W., Washington, D.C., 20036.

In 1972, two case studies were prepared as part of the Rachel Carson Project, with the financial support of the same federal agency. These deal with the Everglades jetport and a proposed dam in Oregon, and are meant for high school or college students. *Case Studies of Two Conservation Battles,* by Virginia Avery and Judith Koerner, 111 pages, available from R. Thomas Tanner, Cispus Environmental Center, Randle, Washington, 98377. $4.00, postpaid. A limited number of copies are available from the author, at cost of printing and mailing.

Seven examples of recent citizen action having environmental benefits are described in *Citizens Make the Difference: Case studies of Environmental Action.* These case studies were not prepared as instructional materials, and we have not yet had the opportunity to review them. The publication is available from the Superintendent of Documents, U.S. Government Printing Office, Washington, D.C., 20402.

The Santa Barbara oil spill is examined in detail in *Blowout,* by Carol E. Steinhart and John S. Steinhart (Belmont, Calif., 94002: Wadsworth Publishing Company, 1972). This is a balanced account of all sides, including the role of government as it tried to cope with the incident. Not prepared as an instructional unit, but could be so used by advanced high school students.

Films

Environmental films are too numerous for separate listing. Lengthy unannotated lists of such films are numerous but of limited value. Instead, here are three annotated lists that we have found useful in our own teaching:

The Environment Film Review. New York: Environment Information Center, Film Reference Department (124 East 39th Street, zip 10016), 1972. The most comprehensive guide available, it reviews 627 films selected from among thousands produced. Gives lengthy critical annotations, purchase and rental prices, distributors' addresses, running time, other pertinent information. Grouped into twenty-one categories, including "Land Use and Misuse" (the most useful category for our interests), "Air Pollution," and "Solid Waste." Look especially at the films rated with one or two stars. Some of the films are on a free-loan basis. The *Review* is to be updated and published annually.

Free-Loan Films: Environment. New Hyde Park, N.Y.: Modern Talking Picture Service (2323 New Hyde Park Road, zip 11040), published occasionally. These free films are all available from MTPS or one of its regional outlets. Order well in advance due to heavy demand. Includes a number of industry films taking a positive, solution-oriented approach; for example, Chevrolet's *A Noble Venture.*

Listings of Interior Environment & Natural Resource Films. Washington, D.C.: U.S. Department of the Interior (zip 20240). Published annually. Describes the free-loan films available from the various bureaus and agencies within Interior.

The editors of the first publication listed above make a very appropriate observation: most of the films available to date constitute what they call "First Generation Environmental Cinema" — superficial finger-pointing at problems. "Second Generation" films, which probe deeper into specific cases and propose solutions, are as yet infrequent.

The teacher may be able to achieve a second-generation situation by selecting films that are more or less opposed on the same issue, using these as the jumping-off spot for a case study. A detailed example of this technique is given in the next chapter. The films available from these three catalogs provide opportunities for this.

The film libraries of large universities are also a source of film rentals at reasonable rates.

Simulations and Games

Many EE simulations have been produced by teachers and others in recent years. These are learning strategies in which students simulate a situation having environmental significance. Often the situation is a public hearing in which a decision-making body is listening to witnesses representing various sides of an issue. Students take the roles of the various parties, and learn by studying and then arguing their positions, or by making decisions based upon the arguments. Most such simulations are based upon fictitious but realistic issues, some are based upon actual ones. A few examples:

ASMUSSEN, DENNIS G., and COLE, RICHARD A. "A Land-Use Alternatives Model for Upper Elementary Environmental Education." *Journal of Geography* (May 1970): 267-72. The children must decide how to use some farmland just outside Centerplace City. They role-play as the town's Board of Control and as various interest groups representing different uses for the land. The article includes all the directions and background information necessary for what looks like a good classroom unit.

KRACHT, JAMES B., and MARTORELLA, PETER H. "Simulation and Inquiry Models Applied to the Study of Environmental Problems." *Journal of Geography* (May 1970): 273-78. The students, as citizens of Pleasantville, must decide what to do about the town's solid waste problem. Interestingly, some of the trash consists of nonreturnable bottles from the Kool-Kola Bottling Company, a local employer. The town's grocers don't want to handle returnable bottles. The local conservation club advocates a boycott of Kool-Kola if they don't convert. Fun.

QUIGLEY, CHARLES N., and LONGAKER, RICHARD P. "Storm King Mountain." Case 3 in *Voices for Justice*. Boston: Ginn, 1970. Pp. 23-34. This role-playing simulation involves an actual case, circa 1967 and after, which pitted a power company against people who wanted to preserve the beauty of the upper Hudson River. For high school and college students. We would suggest that the players prepare for their roles by doing some background reading on this case; see the magazines listed in the *"Case Studies"* section above. *Voices for Justice* contains seven other simulations of actual cases, but these are not directly ecological-environmental in nature.

"The Tussock Moth Issue" was not prepared for commercial distribution but is is an interesting simulation worth mention. It also deals with a real issue: the decision about whether to allow emergency use of DDT on certain forests in the Pacific Northwest, following an outbreak of a tree-killing caterpillar. (The Environmental Protection Agency, in fact, denied the requests for DDT use.) It simulates a public hearing, with students assuming the roles of various witnesses and a decision-making body. Supplemented by a bulletin from the Oregon State University Extension Service and by a letter from the governor of Oregon, it provides instructions, background information, news items and letters with all sides fairly presented. The teaching instructions on page 4-15 and 46-59 are highly structured; the teacher may prefer to use only those on pages 16-19, which were prepared and tested by a classroom teacher. Contact Georgia Pacific Corporation, 900 SW 5th, Portland, Oregon, 97204.

Other simulations are scattered throughout the materials and programs reviewed in this chapter.

Although it is not always easy (or necessary) to distinguish a simulation from a game, the latter may be defined as a device rather more akin to Monopoly or Parchesi—essentially a board game. A number of these have been produced commercially for EE, and for all ages of learners. Their strong points include a high degree of interest and participation on the part of the learner, as with simulations. Disadvantages include the following: games may often be won by gamesmanship rather than by attending to the concepts the game is meant to teach; treatment of concepts is sometimes superficial; instructions are sometimes complex and difficult.

Information on a large number of EE games and simulations, including cost and age level, is found in the following sources:

Ecosources 1, No. 12 (December 1972). Send a stamped, self-addressed envelope to Janet Woerner, Freeland High School, 710 Powley Drive, Freeland, Michigan, 48623. Ms. Woerner compiles *Ecosource* bibliographies on various EE materials from time to time.

PIERFY, DAVID. "Simulation Games." In *The Southeastern Regional Conference on the Social Sciences and Environmental Education.* Athens, Ga.: Department of Social Science Education, University of Georgia (zip 30601), 1971. Pp. 31-36.

Materials for Urban EE

The following three items are a sample of the materials that have been prepared for urban EE. They are reviewed at some length in order to demonstrate the distinctive nature of this class of materials.

A Place to Live, published by the National Audubon Society in 1970, includes a student manual and teacher's manual, both bearing the same title. In this program, apparently designed for intermediate grades, the child explores vestiges of nature in the inner city. The manuals feature ten "walks" in which the child is directed to closely examine and record certain features of the urban environment. Each walk is related to a lesson in the manuals. In the bird lesson, the child is introduced to four birds that have adapted especially well to city life: the English sparrow, the starling, the pigeon, and the gull. On the correlated walk, he records the number of birds seen and their species. He then chooses one species for closer study, and is directed to: "Circle the [drawing of a] bill that looks most like your bird's bill." "Circle the feet that look most like your bird's feet." "Circle the tail. . . ." "Circle the wing. . . ." He is asked: "What color(s) is your bird?" "If your bird was eating, what was he eating?"

On the neighborhood walk, the child draws a map of the several blocks near his school or home and indicates types of buildings with certain symbols—star for school, hammer for factory, and so on. He also orients his map to compass directions. The building walk provides an opportunity for him to discover such phenomena as the pattern of wear on the steps of older buildings and the manner in which streets and sidewalks are both sloped toward the gutter for water run-off. The teacher's manual at this point gives the teacher some assistance in teaching a sort of urban geology lesson, in which the origins of various man-made building materials (porcelain, asphalt) and natural building materials (slate, marble) are examined, though perhaps too briefly. Other walks, lessons, and experiments deal with soil, ants, trees, plants, rain, and animals. Although some urban children may have to search awhile to locate a tree they can examine, the lessons seem realistically geared to that which can be found in the city: the plants examined include grass, dandelions, and moss; the insects include housefly, mosquito, cockroach.

The final walk and lesson deal with the environment. The child looks for evidence of pollution and litter. He is directed, for instance, to "sandpaper a small section of the stones on the outside of the school building. Is there a difference in color?"

This publication grew out of teacher workshops, which the Audubon Society has held in New York City since 1965. Trial editions were tried in the classrooms of teachers who attended the workshops. Thus the program reflects both the commitments of the society and the experience of teachers and children. Contact National Audubon Society, 950 Third Avenue, New York, New York, 10022.

Man's Habitat—The City, is a teacher's manual also published in 1970, apparently for intermediate grades. Unlike the Audubon program, this manual does not deal with the world of nature. Rather, the children are to become very familiar with other aspects of their community and neighborhood. There are three major investigations: "Orientation in the School Community," "Recognizing Relationships," and "Community Profiles." In the first, the children locate their homes on a large projection of a city map. They then discuss such questions as: "In which area do most of the children live?" "Do more children live in apartments than in houses? (raise hands)." "Are these located on certain areas of the map?" They then take a walk similar to the neighborhood walk in the Audubon program, later transferring their information to the large class map. They color-code those parts of the community that are for children and those that are for adults, and mark those places they would go for this-or-that (to buy new shoes, for instance, or to play baseball). In short, the first investigation simply makes them more familiar with their community. In the second investigation, the children again use maps, this time plotting the location of parks and of their own homes to see whether any new parks are needed. Some suggestions are made for actions the class might take to *get* a new park, should they determine that there is a need for one. In the final investigation, the children develop questionnaires and go out into the community to interview people about where they buy their food, how old their homes are, how often the garbage man comes, and the like.

If the children in a class did all of the investigations described, they would become very familiar with their habitats. The final investigation, however, could be a rather messy procedure; the teacher should probably determine whether the children have good reasons for the questions they intend to ask before launching forth into the community. There is also the question of whether the children are to do this investigation on their own time or on school time, a matter not easily dismissed when schools are responsible for the safety and conduct of children. In the second investigation, it would be good to determine where children *do* play, and *what* they play, before proposing a new park. Such information may suggest modifications in existing parks rather than a need for new ones. This program requires a certain amount of preparation time of the teacher, who needs some photocopying and overhead projection capability at hand. Contact the Environmental Science Center, 5400 Glenwood Avenue, Golden Valley, Minnesota, 55422.

Environmental Education on an Urban School Site: A Guide for Teachers was produced by the National Park Service, Pacific Northwest Region, 523 Fourth and Pike Building, Seattle, Washington, 98101. It is a teacher's manual, apparently for intermediate grades, undated. It is not for sale, but is intended for use with the service's teacher workshops. It consists mainly of a potpourri of outdoor investigations borrowed mostly from a variety of sources, including the U.S. Forest Service, local school districts, and the Audubon program described above. These vary in the amount of set-up time required of teachers; many are reasonably undemanding in this regard. The background information provided for studying a dandelion in a sidewalk crack is unusually thorough and detailed. (The background information provided for teachers in much of the new EE material leaves much to be desired.) Some of the ideas are relevant to contemporary environmental problems. For instance, the children fasten down varied samples of modern garbage and litter and observe them over a period of months to see which disappear and which remain undegraded. (One wonders how much will disappear by means *other* than decomposition, though—a stiff breeze or some stray dogs could affect the results on this one.) The children analyze the school's garbage and suggest alternatives to disposal for each kind of item. They discuss the possibility of sharing the family newspaper with another family to save resources and reduce solid waste.

It may be questioned whether some of the investigations are truly urban in nature, for example, those on wildlife and nature trails. However, the urban teacher can pick and choose some useful activities from among those in this book.

Materials from State Education Departments

Some state departments of education have produced materials for teacher use. In 1971 and 1972, Minnesota produced units for teachers of French, German, and Spanish. The lesson plans therein utilize articles, cartoons, and advertisements from foreign-language magazines, and deal with solid waste and recycling, land-use planning, population, pollution, preservation of parklands, and the plight of the polar bear. The lessons are mainly for intermediate and advanced students. Printed by the Minnesota State Department of Education, Capitol Square, St. Paul, Minnesota, 55101. Wisconsin recently produced a volume containing nearly two hundred problems for mathematics, grades 6-9. They deal mainly with pollution and are arranged by categories: whole, rational, and real numbers, percentage and proportion, measurement, statistical measures and graphs. Entitled *Pollution,* the booklet is printed by the Wisconsin Department of Public Instruction, Division of Instructional Services, 126 Langdon Street, Madison, Wisconsin, 53702. Wisconsin has also reprinted the Minnesota foreign-language units and has produced an outline for a one-semester high school course, "Ecology and Human Values," which could be team-taught by teachers of biology and social sciences.

California's department of education has produced some good books on the *theory* of instruction. It did so for science education several years ago, and with the publication of *Ekistics* it did so for EE in 1973. The book is primarily the work of Dr. Paul Brandwein, long an insightful theoretician in EE. *Ekistics* is published by the California State Department of Education, 721 Capitol Mall, Sacramento, California, 95814.

The state of Washington has produced an excellent little volume entitled *Teaching Population Concepts.* It provides a wealth of quantitative background information and teaching suggestions. Published by State Superintendent of Public Instruction, Old Capitol Building, Olympia, Washington, 98504.

The education department of New York State wrote two volumes entitled *EE Instructional Activities K-12.* One volume is for K-6, the other for 7-12. Topics covered include survival, interdependence, scarcity, recycling, rights versus responsibility, planning, valuing, social forces, and optimism. Available from ERIC Document Reproduction Service, Leasco Information Products, Inc., 4827 Rugby Avenue, Bethesda, Maryland, 20014.

The Alaska Department of Education has printed a large number of two- and three-page EE activities representing various subject areas and grade levels. These include student investigations regarding snowmobiles, hunting laws, land planning, paper waste in schools, and identification of Alaska wild berries, among others. They were apparently solicited from teachers around the state. Contact Environmental Education Specialist, Alaska Department of Education, Pouch F, Juneau, Alaska, 99801.

These six states provide just a sample. You may wish to write your own state education department to determine what EE materials it may have available.

Multidisciplinary, Multigrade Curriculum Projects

In recent years a number of EE curriculum projects have been published. These are intended as more or less complete EE programs, and they tend to be multidisciplinary and multigrade, often K-12, sometimes K-6 or K-9. In reviewing such programs, the reader should take careful note of the following three categories:

1. Some EE programs concentrate on EE concepts; they represent more or less disciplined definitions of EE. Their materials are meant to be integrated into the teacher's regular courses in language arts, science, or whatever.
2. Some programs in the various disciplines are not called EE programs, but they nevertheless incorporate some EE concepts into their materials. An excellent example is the SCIS science program for grades 1-6, which develops the concepts of ecosystem, populations, and communities of living things.
3. Some programs are *called* EE programs but otherwise fit description (2) above. They include many concepts or activities not clearly related to EE. It is up to the teacher to decide whether such a program represents a good integration of EE into other subject areas or simply an undisciplined, unfocused view of EE.

The following programs represent a random sampling of categories (1) and (3); no endorsement of these programs is implied or intended.

The Scholastic *Earth Corps Study Program* includes six multimedia units, three for social studies and three for science. The units are activity-oriented and may be used sequentially through grades 1-6 to reinforce the same basic concepts in an increasingly sophisticated manner as grade level increases. Each grade-level unit has specific learning goals and lists concepts to be developed by each lesson in the unit. Contact Scholastic Book Services, 904 Sylvan Avenue, Englewood Cliffs, New Jersey, 07632.

The National Park Service is preparing a K-12 multidisciplinary program with lessons in art, music, mathematics, social studies, language arts, and science. One feature setting this apart from some other programs is that the music, art, and language arts activities are not based entirely on self-expression: the children experience the beautiful works of others, as well. Materials for grades 3-6 are available to date. For grades 5-6 there is an outdoor book for use in a one-week resident outdoor school, a correlated classroom book for use during the remainder of the school year, and a teacher's guide. For grades 3-4 there are a classroom book and a teacher's guide. These are attractively presented materials with many good photos and illustrations of artistic expression. The books are entitled *Adventure in Environment*, the overall program is called NEED (National Environmental Education Development). Contact National Park Service, Department of the Interior, Washington, D.C., 20240.

In South Carolina, in 1966 and 1967, the Conservation Curriculum Improvement Project involved some thirty-four teachers in writing lessons to represent a spectrum of subjects and grade levels. These have been published nationally in eight volumes. The K-12, multidisciplinary nature of the project is suggested by the volume titles: *Social Studies 7-8-9* and *Social Studies 10-11-12; 9-12 Home Economics; Science 7-8-9; Biology; Grades 1-2-3* and *Grades 4-5-6; 1-12 Outdoor Laboratory.* The lessons were subjected to classroom trial and revision, and the project had excellent consultants — Drs. Paul Brandwein and Matthew J. Brennan. Individual lessons seem to reflect the efforts of individual teacher-writers, who apparently represented a spectrum of knowledge and ability. The lessons are built around three major concepts of Dr. Brandwein's: (1) living things are interdependent with one another and with their environment; (2) organisms (or populations of organisms) are the product of their heredity and environment; (3) organisms and environments are in constant change. Contact J. G. Ferguson Publishing Company, 6 North Michigan Avenue, Chicago, Illinois, 60602.

The AEP Ecology Program includes materials for grades K-12. The *Focus on Pollution* series examines the kinds, causes, effects, and solutions of environmental ills. This series is written for K-3, and is continued as the AEP Ecology program in grades 4-6. This intermediate program is developed around four basic concepts — diversity, adaptation, interrelationships, and change; it attempts to develop an environmental ethic. The secondary portion of this program divides ecology into four broad areas — Diversity, Adaptation, Interrelationships, and Succession — and is built around a two-part series entitled *You and Your Environment* for grade 7-9 and supplemental reading in three other pamphlets: *Ecology: Man Explores Life* (7-9), *Our Polluted World* (7-12), and *The Conservation Story* (7-12). This program is primarily science and social studies centered. Contact American Education Publications, Columbus, Ohio, 43216.

The materials from Project I-C-E in Green Bay, Wisconsin, are available from ERIC Document Reproduction Service, Leasco Information Products, Inc., 4827 Rugby Avenue, Bethesda, Maryland, 20014. There are three volumes, one each for social studies, language arts, and science. These contain K-12 lessons developed and tried by over a hundred teachers. Objectives are in both the cognitive and affective domains; learning activities occur both in class and in the community.

The program of the North Jersey Conservation Foundation is bound in four volumes — one for grades 1-3, and one each for grades 4, 5, 6. Entitled *Education for Survival: Ecology in Science and Social Studies.* Contact NJCF, 300 Mendham Road, Morristown, New Jersey.

The National Wildlife Federation has published a series of student investigations for grades K-9. Some of the units are, for instance, "Stream Profiles" (grades 4-9), "Nature's Part in Art" (3-6), "Plant Puzzles" (1-6), "Genetic Variation" (4-9), "Sampling Button Populations" (3-9). Called the *Environmental Discovery Series*, and prepared by Minnesota Environmental Sciences Foundation. Contact NWF, Educational Servicing, 1412 16th Street, NW, Washington, D.C., 20036.

The Environmental Studies kit includes seventy-five assignment cards and explanatory materials; additional booklets and posters are available. The learner uses each activity card to explore some feature of his own environment, including his feelings and perceptions. In a classroom situation, individuals or small groups may work on the same or different tasks simultaneously. Typical activities include the following: (1) tape-recording sounds that evoke certain emotions, such as sadness; (2) creating pieces of art from materials found in the environment, with each piece illustrating a quality of the environment, such as ugliness or beauty; (3) finding a series of events in which one causes the next, it the next, and so on; (4) going out to observe indirect evidence of a population of something.

This project has been primarily concerned with methodology rather than content, and with the affective more than the cognitive domain. It encourages the teacher to maintain an open classroom, an informal and trusting atmosphere in which the students use the assignment cards as one vehicle in exploring their own "environments." Ideally, students are to choose their own objectives and grade their own performance. (However, a teacher can still use the assignment cards even if he does not accept this philosophy entirely.) This project has never defined or limited the scope of that which it considers to be "environmental studies." Furthermore, it has, during its progress, moved steadily away from its origins as an EE project. For instance, the first fifty assignments, developed in 1970-71, tend to have the learner exploring the world "out there." In the last twenty-five, developed in 1972, he is more often exploring his own feelings and perceptions, and those of others. It is interesting that the word *environment* appears seventeen times in the first fifty assignments, and only once in the last twenty-five.

Those who feel that *urban* EE must consist of exploring the immediate environment will find these materials very useful. So will others. The assignments do stimulate a high degree of involvement and activity among those using them, as we can testify from personal experience and observation. The philosophy of the project is well argued in the booklets included in the kit, and the assignment cards are consistent with the philosophy.

Many of the tasks are consistent with, and could easily be a part of, a total EE program. For instance, the chain of causal relationships found by some students might be industry ⟶ pollution ⟶ "No Swimming" signs. Or more positively, it might be aroused citizens ⟶ appeal to city council ⟶ reduction of industrial effluents and recycling of the former "waste" materials.

Thus the ES project materials could be part of an overall EE program, but it will help if the teacher is clever and knowledgeable. The materials do not constitute an entire EE program, especially for students who proceed reasonably well under more traditional school conditions. Contact Environmental Studies Project, American Geological Institute, Box 1559, Boulder, Colorado, 80302.

In addition to the curriculum projects above, there is a plethora of instructional materials intended not as an entire program but as supplementary materials for one subject area and one or a few grade levels. Some of these are excellent, and used in concert they could do much for a school's K-12 multidisciplinary program. One should contact publishers' sales representatives to see what they have in this regard. Also see the Helgeson publication cited below.

This chapter has included just a small sampling of EE programs and materials, including some noteworthy projects that have not yet attracted much attention. Descriptions of additional programs and materials can be found in:

HELGESON, STANLEY L., et al. *A Review of Environmental Education for Elementary and Secondary School Teachers.* Bethesda, Md.: ERIC Document Reproduction Service, Leasco Information Products (4827 Rugby Avenue, zip 20014), 1971. ED No. 059 913; paper or microfiche.

Inquiries may also be directed to the ERIC/SMEAC Center, which can provide information on a variety of topics in EE. Address: 400 Lincoln Tower, Ohio State University, Columbus, Ohio, 43210.

CHAPTER 4

Professional Development in Environmental Education

A TEACHER WORKSHOP IN EE

"The major objective of the workshop is for you to complete – or maybe just begin – a project which will be useful to you personally. For most of you this will probably be a lesson or a unit to use in one of your classes. For some of you it may simply be that you will catch up on a lot of reading appropriate to EE. We have a wealth of reading matter here for you, as I'll show you soon. There will be some lecture-discussion sessions on most days, but never for more than an hour or two a day. We don't believe that being talked at is necessarily the only way to learn. The rest of the time will be yours. We will be here to point out materials that may be useful to you as individuals, or to assist you in any other way we can. We want you to look upon these two weeks as a dynamic retreat: a *retreat* in that you will be removed from the score of daily interruptions that interfere with work and contemplation back home; *dynamic* in that you'll have a rich learning environment – you won't lack for materials to stimulate your thinking.

"Here in this section we have current curriculum projects in EE – every program we've heard of is represented here. There are lessons and teaching ideas for every grade level and most subject areas. Some of you may simply pick and choose among these as your project. That'll be fine. Over here are background books – not education books *per se* – but works having to do with our environmental-ecological situation. Some are mainly science-oriented, some social-science, and some are beautiful literature. Let me point out a few of these to you. . . ."

Thus begins a summer workshop offered by Central Washington State College at the Cispus Environmental Learning Center in the Cascade Mountains of Washington. The twenty-nine teachers present, mostly elementary teachers, will spend the next two weeks working

in the kind of atmosphere indicated by the instructor's opening remarks. Almost all will work diligently on projects of their own choice.
Many will create EE lessons or choose from among those made available. An elementary-school teacher will revise some field investigations used by his school when it visits Cispus during the year. Two
school librarians will compile selected "shopping lists" for next
year's book order. A high school home economics teacher will create
some lesson plans, using books and articles which the instructional
staff has collected for her specific subject area. One elementary principal will prepare the detailed agenda for an informal EE workshop
in her own school. A fifth-grade teacher who has many American Indian students will tape-record a number of Northwest Indian legends
illustrating the relationship the Indian had with the world of nature.

During the two weeks, the workshop participants will place a
heavy demand on the books that emerge as their favorites: The angry
and beautiful essays of Abbey's *Desert Solitaire;* John McPhee's
unique *Encounters with the Archdruid,* recounting conversations and
adventures shared by conservationist David Brower and three of his
"natural enemies": a developer, a mining-engineer, a dam builder;
The Sense of Wonder, in which Rachel Carson tells us how — and why
— to take nature walks with children; *A Sand County Almanac* by
Aldo Leopold, and *Blueprint for Survival;* Fred Bodsworth's novel,
The Last of the Curlews ("I cried," admitted some. "Good, you just
passed the course," replied the instructor).

Almost all the teachers will take a day's field trip over the top of
Burley Mountain, to Mosquito Meadows and back. The overt reason
will be to observe a few life zones and geological features. The covert
reason will be to allow their own sense of wonder to deepen, as they
travel a high road where no cars or other people will be seen all day.
During part of the workshop's unstructured time, many will walk,
some will hike, a few will float the Cispus River on inner tubes. ("Gee,
I never walked through woods slowly before, without some objective
I was trying to reach. It was a whole new experience," said one.
"Good, you just passed the course," replied the instructor.)

At the end of the workshop, most will have a much more sophisticated view of EE than they had previously. Several will confer with
the instructors regarding the possibility of the latter offering workshops back in their home communities during the next school year.
And, on an anonymous evaluation form, twenty-four will rate the
workshop "excellent," five "good," none "average," "fair," or "poor."
Almost all will volunteer the comment that they enjoyed the high degree of freedom to work on EE projects significant to them personally.

Let us examine more closely the few lecture-discussions of this example teacher-education program to see what experiences all the participants had in common.

The instructor begins one early session with these words: "In a minute I want you to break up into small groups. There, you are to come up with policies and laws which the nations of the world must institute, immediately and over the long haul, to reach the following objective: that all peoples of the world, five hundred years from now, will be able to live at reasonable levels of dignity, comfort, and good physical and mental health. Furthermore, these conditions will continue to prevail for an indefinite future after that. OK—go to it; I'll come around with more instructions later."

After a half-hour, the instructor interjects this comment into each group: "I perceive that you are having a procedural problem, and here is the answer. You find yourselves having to choose between political reality—what governments *will* do immediately—and ecological reality—what they *should* do. Right? OK, for our purposes, choose ecological reality. Ignore political reality. See you in a while."

After another half-hour of discussion, each group is briefly introduced to the book *Blueprint for Survival*. They learn that the authors of *Blueprint* ran into the same problem they did. So the *Blueprint* authors opted for ecological reality, leaving compromise to others. Then they receive summaries of *Blueprint* similar to the one found in the Introduction to this book. They are instructed, "In about twenty minutes we'll reconvene, at which time I'll ask each group's spokesman—choose one—to tell the total group two things: a recommendation made by your group but not by *Blueprint*, and one made by *Blueprint* but not by your group."

In this lesson there are two objectives: (1) The students should engage in long-range, Spaceship Earth thinking—some, probably, for the first time; (2) They should learn what some authorities have thought in this regard. The sequence of events used in the lesson is based upon the instructors' belief that the participants will learn most from (2) by sharing the experience of earth-planning with the authorities.

Another lesson lasts one entire morning, but with a variety of activities and ample "stretching time." The participants are handed a set of discussion questions for two half-hour films which are to follow:

1. Do the two films represent different value systems? Pick out specific words used by each narrator, or other clues, that will illustrate your answer.

2. If two value systems are represented, will they come into conflict more often in future than they have in the past? Why or why not?

3. Is such conflict limited to dams?

4. Important question. It may take you two weeks to decide upon an answer: What criteria should be used in resolving such conflict in future?

5. Discuss any other important question we have failed to ask you.

"Notice," says the instructor, "that these are printed on one-third of a sheet of paper. We're saving trees.

"Now, everything we'll do this morning deals with one specific case study. There's an excellent reason for this. By now you and your students have been well exposed to the generalized problems of pollution and population. The media are full of belching smokestacks and belly-up fish, and the kids are saturated with it. They all have a superficial exposure to our environmental dilemma; there's no point in your exposing them to more of that. They're now overdue for some case studies of specific issues, examined much more closely. Some of you teach very young children, to whom these comments may not apply. But all of us, as adults and teachers, will better understand EE if we look at some specific cases.

"The two films you're about to see deal with the Glen Canyon Dam in Utah. The first is from the Bureau of Reclamation, the second is from the Sierra Club. If you know anything about these two organizations you already suspect the truth—the two films are not in complete agreement. OK, let's roll 'em."

The first film details the building of Glen Canyon Dam across the Colorado River. The narrator places great emphasis upon such words as *power, mighty, great*. The second film shows the side canyons off Glen, as they appeared prior to the dam. They are like nothing seen anywhere else, some being hundreds of feet deep and only a few feet across, carved down through the desert rock. The film then shows the mud and debris collected in them by the rising waters behind the dam. At the film's conclusion, any sensitive person is likely to experience a great feeling of loss. The film is done very quietly, in a low-key style.

After the films, the students break into small groups to discuss the questions, without further comment by the instructor. Later, they reconvene for a brief large-group discussion of the questions. Some are sympathetic with one side, some with the other, most are perplexed. The instructor avoids taking sides. Instead, he introduces the next film with the following words:

"You're seeing the films in chronological order of production, and this next film was produced by the Bureau of Reclamation in response to the Sierra Club film which you last saw. Now something to notice here is the nature of the appeal that is made. Often, the opposing groups on an issue like this will adopt the type of appeal made by the opponent. For instance, opponents of groups like the Sierra Club and the Wilderness Society have always accused them of being elitists, of wanting wilderness locked up for the pleasure of a few rich people instead of being developed for the economic gain of the many. Well, in a few days you'll see a recent Sierra Club film, which adopts the enemy strategy, as it were.[1] It will suggest that Grand Canyon be preserved for the many instead of dammed for the economic gain of comparatively few.

"You're going to see the same kind of switch now. In the last film, the Sierra Club appealed to your love of nature, your esthetic sensibilities. Well, now the bureau is going to do the same."

The film which follows shows the beauties of Lake Powell, created by Glen Canyon Dam. It follows a family as they explore the side canyons by boat and by foot.

After the film and a stretch break, the instructor resumes: "Often, in these battles, both sides will present the facts as they perceive them, leaving persons like you and me wondering just where the truth lies. Sometimes the conservation groups may exaggerate the bad effects of a proposed project. Sometimes the developer may omit or ignore real dangers and relevant facts. Consider the films you've seen. In the Sierra Club film, we saw the filmmakers exploring some interesting Indian ruins near the upper end of the proposed Lake Powell. Perhaps the implication, by association, is that those would be covered with water. But I don't know whether they would be, since they're near the upper end of the lake. I do know this. In the film you just saw, in which you were shown the beauty that still remains in the side canyons, there was an omission. The bureau neglected to tell you that the dam hadn't yet been filled. It still had more than two hundred feet to go. Remember the scenes of Rainbow Bridge National Monument? No lake in sight. Right? If the dam is filled, the water of Lake Powell will be at the foot of the bridge. Obviously, that will change the character of the scenes you saw. The Sierra Club says it will also speed erosion at the base of the bridge and cause it to fall soon. Are they right? I don't know. Remember when the family took its boat into Cathedral in the Desert? Before the dam you could walk there, now you could take your boat there. But imagine Cathedral with two hundred more feet of water. Right! No more Cathedral.

"Now I'd like to give you some background on this case, and then get you updated on it."

The instructor goes on to explain two changes which occurred in the conservation movement in the 1950s, both as a result of a newly affluent society with time and money to take to the out-of-doors. First, conservation changed from a utilitarian to an esthetic concern. Dam building, for example, which had been viewed widely as good conservation in the thirties and forties, now began to be opposed effectively by citizen groups interested in wilderness recreation and preservation. Second, conservation changed from a strictly professional to a more popular concern. Citizen groups began to convince a growing audience that the government agencies charged with protecting and developing the nation's natural resources were in need of closer surveillance by a wider segment of the public.

The instructor discusses the landmark, turning-point case: that of the proposed Echo Park dam, in which "archdruid" David Brower led opposition against such foes as Secretary of the Interior Douglas "Give Away" McKay, a former automobile dealer from Oregon.[2]

Finally, he brings the Glen Canyon issue up to date by explaining that today, more than ten years after completion of the dam, it still has not been filled. Recently, conservation groups successfully enjoined the bureau from filling the canyon because, in flooding a national monument, it would break the law. In response, two Utah congressmen initiated bills to change that law. The instructor makes available news articles and other literature on the issue, obtained from both sides in the controversy.[3] He points out that one section of John McPhee's *Encounters with the Archdruid* is directly pertinent to this case,[4] as is one chapter of Edward Abbey's *Desert Solitaire*.[5] He distributes availability information on the films used this morning, pointing out that they can all be obtained free of charge.[6]

He solicits suggestions from the teachers as to how or whether their own students could take a case study further—what would follow an introduction like this one? He concludes by pointing out the teacher's responsibility to remain neutral and objective when dealing with controversy. He reminds them of his own efforts to do so, while admitting, "The more I learn about these cases, however, the harder I find it to be neutral."

By now it is slightly past lunchtime, and the lesson is concluded. During the following days many of the teachers will read the special materials on this issue, as well as McPhee and Abbey. A few evenings later they will also gain some historical perspective on the broader issue of dams in the United States by viewing the film *The River*, produced in 1937 by the Department of Agriculture.[7] *The River* shows the impoverished condition of the land and the people in the Tennessee and lower Mississippi River watersheds at the time. The film concludes by showing the new dams of the Tennessee Valley Authority, which were to improve these conditions markedly. Thus *The River* demonstrates emphatically why conservation was once more utilitarian, less esthetic, as befitted a depression-ridden people living in a deforested, eroded land. Yet the esthetics of the film itself, with its beautiful musical score, powerful cinematography and film editing, and epic narration make their mark upon the group.

Other sessions during the two weeks will include the following: Guest instructor Jim Unterwegner of the Forest Service will lead a trip through the upper Cispus River Valley. Following that, he will divide the teachers into work teams that will plan a future for the valley, trying to accommodate the competing demands of recreationists, the lumber industry, and others. Tom Eckman, the associate instructor for the workshop, will engage the teachers in a number of value clarification activities suitable for classroom use, pointing out the effect that values have on resource use and environmental perception. The instructional team will run the teachers through some field investigations designed to represent: (1) a reasonable mix of the affective, cognitive, and psychomotor domains, and (2) an enjoyable and satisfying degree of inquiry by the learner. The team will explain in detail a list of criteria for evaluating EE materials. There will be environmental "film festivals" on several evenings. Selected articles will be set out for the teachers to browse through at their leisure. Some of these will be good news, such as Union-Camp Corporation's gift to the nation of a fifty-thousand-acre wilderness. Some will be what the team calls "hair curlers" — examples of backlash against the new environmentalism, including reports of alleged reprisals against those who have spoken out on behalf of the environment. The principal instructor will conduct a short lecture on "audacious concepts" such as:

1. Culture Lag as Environmental Deteriorator in *All* Cultures;
2. Margin for Error, or — We Cannot Avoid *Some* Environmental Errors, but We can Absorb Them Better If We're Not SRO ["Standing Room Only"];
3. The Popular Misconcept of Equally Shared Guilt, or, Would *You* Send the Company Jet Back from Europe to Texas for a Gown You'd Forgotten?

The above description of one workshop for teachers has been set forth in some detail for a number of reasons.

First, it illustrates many of the issues discussed elsewhere in this book. For instance, the instructional team attended to both the *content* and the *methodology* of EE. That is, the *scope* or *definition* of EE was set within reasonable bounds — man-earth relationships provided the focus — yet the participants were given complete freedom to choose their own objectives and work toward them in their own way. The workshop was open to teachers of *all subjects and grade levels;* the experiences common to all of them — the lecture-discussions — were meant to provide them with a philosophical groundwork that would serve as the necessary base for sound EE practice, regardless of the specific subject to be taught. There was emphasis on *affective* as well as *cognitive* (and psychomotor) learning, with time to indulge all the domains in an unhurried manner. There was a determined effort to present *all sides of controversial issues,* and to present *good news* as well as bad.

Second, this workshop illustrates the case-study approach in EE and some reasons for using case studies of specific issues.

Third, it suggests some materials and techniques that the reader may wish to adapt for his own classroom.

Fourth, it illustrates the significant subject matter with which EE must deal, at a time when there is real danger that EE will be frittered away on the frivolous. Many participants in the workshops offered by this instructional team have commented that their eyes were opened to a whole new world of issues, concepts, and world-views to which they had not been previously exposed, although several had taken EE workshops stressing field-trip techniques or other matters. These persons viewed the two kinds of workshops as being complementary to each other.

Fifth, it serves to introduce the next topic.

TEACHER EDUCATION PROGRAMS IN EE

For practicing teachers, there are or have been a smattering of various kinds of EE workshops and inservice courses available around the country. We will sample a few of these and then go on to some comments regarding preservice programs for undergraduates in education.

In 1971, the School of Education at the City College of New York initiated a fifteen-week course for teachers representing all grades and subject levels. Following an introduction to the literature on environmental issues, the teachers do research on a specific problem and are encouraged to go on to appropriate political action. The instructor's philosophy is that controversial issues should not be shied away from, and the scope of what he considers as environmental problems seems generally appropriate. This single course has since expanded into a graduate program offering the M.A. in Environmental Education.

The University of Cincinnati offers high school teachers a summer institute on population education. The teachers develop their own teaching materials; lectures and discussions deal with the history of the population problem, the carrying capacity of the earth, and approaches to self-regulation. The institute is team-taught by professors representing biology and various of the social sciences.

The Huxley Center for Environmental Education at Western Washington State College offers separate summer institutes for elementary teachers and for high school science teachers. The latter study: techniques of environmental measurements, such as the levels of pollutants in streams; ways of relating their discipline to the social studies and other areas; an individually selected case study of an environmental problem in the Pacific Northwest. The elementary teachers examine regional case studies, review curriculum materials, and receive a general introduction to EE.

The National Audubon Society has instructed several hundred New York City elementary teachers in methods of "urban ecology." The instructional materials used in this program are described in Chapter 3.

The Massachusetts and Seattle chapters of Zero Population Growth, a volunteer organization, have offered successful weekend workshops for teachers on population education.

In 1971, ten graduate students in the Yale University School of Forestry initiated an EE course for elementary and secondary teachers. The Yale students took the teachers and fourteen hundred of their students on several field trips, each of which was devoted to a specific concept. The teachers developed lessons of their own, were made acquainted with a variety of instructional materials, and heard lectures on such topics as "Endangered Species" and "Consumerism and Wastes."

It is a conspicuous fact that only one of the programs in the random sample above was initiated by a department of education in a college or university. Not only is this indicative of the status of inservice courses for practicing teachers, it is probably even more true of preservice programs for undergraduate education students. In 1968, one researcher did a survey of environmental studies in various departments and schools in twenty-four American universities. One of his several conclusions was that perhaps the most serious shortcoming observed in the entire study "was the absence of any vigorous EE program in the Departments or Schools of Education. . . . Overall a very modest and uncoordinated teacher training effort in the area of EE was the rule at every institution studied in the inventory."[8]

In a more recent study—limited to environmental science—another researcher found that only 19 percent of the universities in his sample offered a course in methods of teaching environmental science. The survey was done in 1970; it was repeated in 1972, with identical results.[9]

Thus, examples of EE courses for preservice education students are not easily located. It has more often been the case that interested professors have incorporated EE into their existing courses. Each term the social science teachers of Dr. J. D. McAulay at Penn State develop teaching units around a specific topic. On several occasions the topic has been environmental-ecological in nature. In his methods and curriculum courses in the Department of Education at North Texas State University, Dr. Clifford Hardy teaches his students the use of various teaching methods, such as simulations, role-playing, the setting of general and specific objectives, lesson planning, and the like. These are typical procedures of education courses. But Dr. Hardy uses environmental topics as the examples, or vehicles, to develop these teaching skills in his students. The teaching units he has used include "The Population Explosion," "The Hidden Cost of Power," and "A Mock Trial" (of a polluting industry). Most of the 240 students so far enrolled in the classes report that they intend to develop detailed environmental units in their own teaching.

An educator like Dr. Hardy illustrates the philosophy of the Rachel Carson Project, which was discussed earlier. That is, EE is incorporated into his regular courses with no change of course title and with no sacrifice of the original course objectives, which in this case were the conveying of certain teaching skills.

The slowness of schools of education to offer preservice programs or courses in EE is not hard to understand. The environment has been a widely popular issue for only a few years, and it is not clear whether it will remain such. State requirements for certification of teachers cannot be changed that quickly, which is perhaps just as well, lest programs be in constant flux and confusion in response to current social issues. Also, EE is just one concern among many which compete for the attention of college deans, legislators, state boards of education, and others who determine certification requirements. Finally, such policymakers are not yet sure what the nature of such changes should be. Leaders in EE agree that EE should be K-12 multidisciplinary, which might suggest at least one EE course for *all* undergraduates. But EE is still perceived by many in education as an intermediate-grade, one-week, outdoor school experience, which would suggest, at most, a course for those preparing to be elementary teachers at the intermediate grade levels. So, for a time at least, most teacher education projects in EE will continue to aim at experienced teachers, and will often be initiated outside the schools of education.

This brings us to the next issue.

SOME NOTES ON THE STATUS OF EE

In February 1972, Dr. John Trent of the University of Nevada surveyed the fifty state departments of education regarding EE. He received some interesting but not surprising information from the forty-four states that responded. Only fifteen had a full-time EE coordinator in the state department; eight provided EE funds to schools; twenty-five felt their state EE programs were "poorly" financed, six "fairly well," thirteen "not at all," none "extremely well." Of the forty-four, some twenty-seven estimated that fewer than 10 percent of the teachers in their respective states had received preservice or inservice instruction in EE.[10]

In the past, the federal government made an effort to supply some funds to EE where local and state funds were not sufficiently available. One major source of federal funding for EE projects was the Elementary and Secondary Education Act of 1965, which supported such worthwhile programs as those at Shawnee Mission, Topeka, Milwaukee, and Nolde Forest Center in Pennsylvania. This massive federal program included a provision of funds for innovative school programs. It was intended that federal funds would get such programs underway; after that the support was to come from local monies. However, cutbacks in federal funds in recent years have been accompanied by tightened pursestrings at the state and local levels. Hence, some programs have withered on the vine.[11]

A more recent federal law, the Environmental Education Act (EEA) of 1970, has shown promise of encouraging sophisticated programs, despite a too-meager budget. For example, the projects of the

Institute for Environmental Education and the National Association for Environmental Education (see Selected Bibliography), as well as the Rachel Carson and Atlanta projects, were all supported with EEA monies. Unfortunately, EEA is itself a case study in the current status of economics and politics. It was passed overwhelmingly by Congress; the Office of Environmental Education created by it was to disburse $45 million over a three-year period to support worthy program proposals. But during the three years since 1970 the administration released only $6.6 of the $45 million. This allowed the funding of fewer than three hundred proposals out of forty-six hundred received during the three-year period. Many proposals of high caliber could not be supported. In an outspoken report, the office's Advisory Council scored the Executive Branch severely on several counts, noting the ability and dedication of the office staff in the face of "considerable harassment" from the Administration. It noted that the President had not requested extension of the act, and expressed its hope that Congress would extend the act in any case. (The matter is before Congress at the time of writing.) The council concluded that "EE has received little more than lip service from the Executive Branch," despite "rhetoric" to the contrary.[12]

An ironic benefit of the above problems is the determination and the knowledge found among many of those now promoting EE. Had the field been better funded, as were many educational efforts early in the 1960s, many people with far less dedication would have moved into EE, and probably would have produced ill-conceived programs. We can only hope that those responsible for some of today's better programs will be around if and when times are better.

This suggests the next important issue:

JOBS IN EE

Clearly, the current status of EE is not encouraging. This statement applies also to the job market in EE, a matter of concern and interest to many young people today. However, our environmental problems have not lessened in recent years, nor will they in the predictable future. If we choose to overcome them humanely and sensibly, EE will inevitably come into its own.

When it does, however, the young person will wish to consider seriously how he can best contribute to it. Much that has been said here suggests that there will be—and possibly should be—a limited market for EE specialists as such. Instead, many will fulfill an important role as ecology-minded classroom teachers—of science, of industrial arts, of physical education, of all the subject areas in which EE can be appropriately introduced. And there are no subject areas in which it cannot.

Some institutions now offer degree programs in something called EE. More may emerge. Some of these programs will include teacher certification requirements, some will not. Young persons should consider this factor in choosing a program. Not only are teaching certificates required of classroom teachers, but most directors of EE in school districts that have EE programs are certificated personnel with classroom experience. It is this writer's impression, however, that opportunities for uncertificated persons vary from one section of the country to another; this factor should be checked out by the aspiring EE specialist.

ORGANIZATIONS IN EE

The teacher interested in EE may wish to join a professional organization whose members share his interests. Following is a list of groups in which membership is open at nominal cost to students, teachers, and others:

National Association for Environmental Education, Box 1295, Miami, Florida, 33143. (Producers of the "Man and Environment" syllabus—see Selected Bibliography.)

American Society for Environmental Education, Curry College, Milton, Massachusetts, 02186.

Conservation Education Association. Contact: Robert O. Ellingson, Department of Natural Resources, Box 450, Madison, Wisconsin, 53701, or David C. Engleson, Department of Public Instruction, 126 Langdon Street, Madison, Wisconsin, 53702.

Association for Environmental and Outdoor Education, 2428 Walnut Boulevard, Walnut Creek, California, 94596, or 5630 200th SW, Apartment B316, Lynnwood, Washington, 98036. A West Coast organization.

As yet, these are small organizations. However, a number of such EE groups are in the process of forming an "Alliance for Environmental Education," which would enable a salaried professional staff to supplement the voluntary labor of the dedicated individuals who now make these groups function.

Some of the EE organizations are quite new, some are older. The older ones in some cases have changed their scope and even their names in response to recent interest in EE.

One should expect to find a full range of sophistication among the members and even among the leaders of these organizations. That is, while some display a good understanding of the objectives of contemporary EE, some do not.

Readers may also be interested in some of the many citizens' groups dedicated to protecting the environment. Examples follow:

The Nature Conservancy, 1800 N. Kent Street, Arlington, Virginia, 22209. One of the most exciting and effective such groups in America, TNC uses various techniques to preserve unspoiled lands. A few of its accomplishments: a 10,000-acre redwood forest in California; a 50,000-acre wilderness in Virginia; a 27,000-acre elk range in Montana—in all, 374,576 acres in 952 projects since 1954. (That's equal to a square plot of ground more than twenty-four miles on each side. Every dollar contributed to TNC saves forty dollars worth of land.)

Environmental Defense Fund, 162 Old Town Road, East Setauket, New York, 11733. With a professional staff of lawyers and others, EDF takes to the courts with suits regarding DDT, supertankers, and a range of environmental problems.

African Wildlife Leadership Foundation, 1717 Massachusetts Avenue, Washington, D.C., 20036. AWLF regards the great African herds as a heritage of all men everywhere. It supports wildlife research and provides training, facilities, and equipment for African wildlife specialists, such as game wardens, wildlife education officers, and others.

National Audubon Society, National Wildlife Federation, and the Wilderness Society. Addresses for these groups are found under "Case Studies" in Chapter 3. Despite their names or original objectives, today they are concerned not just with birds, wildlife, or wilderness, but with the broad range of environmental problems that threaten the objects of their original interest.

CONTROVERSIAL ISSUES IN THE CLASSROOM

EE has great potential for controversy. Its implications touch the pocketbooks of all, the religious beliefs of many. There are three approaches that teachers can use with potentially controversial issues: Hands Off, Soapbox, and Balanced Exposure. The first we deem unacceptable. The widespread charge that education has become irrelevant stems from an excessive use of the Hands Off approach—that is, the avoidance of potentially controversial issues. The Soapbox approach is also unacceptable. Strong advocacy of a single point of view, or attempted indoctrination, challenges the learner's right to develop as a thinking person who weighs evidence and makes rational decisions for himself. Also, this approach may get a teacher fired if his particular dogma runs counter to that of the community. Balanced Exposure, by contrast, finds the teacher remaining objective and open to opposing arguments, finds him and/or the students gathering evidence and arguments from all sides. A very real issue is whether the teacher should try to remain absolutely neutral or should explain the direction of his personal biases to the students—not as advocacy, but as honesty. Both approaches are practiced.

A guest editorial in the *Journal of Environmental Education* has argued that in the absence of a clear national policy, it is inappropriate for a teacher supported by public funds to try to shape attitudes in a specific direction. Yet an issue as sensitive as birth control might well be approached by "providing objective information about the trade-offs implicit in current population growth along with available personal alternatives." The writer of the editorial uses another example to distinguish between what we have called the Balanced Exposure and Soapbox approaches: "Are we trying to teach students about the social costs, benefits, opportunities, and alternatives affected by wilderness preservation or the lack of it? or that wilderness is inherently good and any other alternative is *per se* bad?"[13]

There is a most important distinction between these two approaches to the topic of wilderness preservation, and it should be carried further: In an article entitled "Freedom and a Varied Environment," the present writer pointed out that while there may not be a clear national mandate for wilderness preservation, there is a traditional and constitutional veneration of freedom of choice. There is clearly a restriction of freedom in a national environment where the only available habitats are highly man-altered ones. Plainly, there is greater freedom of choice if one may also choose to work or play in wilderness, rural communities, or other uncrowded and non-metropolitan settings. In short, there is more freedom in a varied environment. The implications for population growth and economic growth are perfectly clear. Examination of many environmental issues will reveal that the defense of the environment rests on venerable American values, especially those of freedom and equality before the law. These "conservative" rationales are not easily rejected by any segment of the political spectrum, or by those who fail to see the inherent good in wilderness *per se.* The teacher wishing to maintain a relevant course of study might keep this in mind.[14]

He should also know that he has the support of the professional education community. For instance, the respected (and certainly not very radical) Association for Supervision and Curriculum Development of the National Education Association had this to say as long ago as 1948: "The school is obligated to make the facts of resources known; to make the possible choices and consequences clear, and to guide individuals to establish sets of values which will balance immediate gain against future need and private riches against social good."[15] No rejection of the Hands Off approach could be clearer!

With local exceptions, the climate for dealing with environmental-ecological issues has improved greatly in recent years. For instance, there is now common acceptance of overpopulation as a problem to be solved; this was not true a decade or two ago. Significantly, issues can now be argued on esthetic as well as economic grounds. One or two decades ago, one was regarded as peculiar if he defended that which was serene or magnificent strictly on the grounds that it was so. The only admissible question at one time seemed to be, Can we make a dollar from it? This change is probably a natural one in a populace that has grown accustomed to affluence, is frustrated by suburbanization, and is seeking weekend satisfaction and recreation "away from the madding crowd."[16]

We may also be moving toward a time when the ethical argument will also be extended. That is, growing numbers of people are saying that objects other than man have rights; that we must act ethically toward beings that are defenseless against us, such as trees, turtles, and tigers. This again is a natural step, since over the long haul of history—with regional and temporary exceptions—man has extended rights to more and more humans. The extension to nonhumans and to inanimate objects—such as mountains and rivers—is the next logical step.

Those who are interested in the entire issue of relevance and controversial issues in the schools may wish to locate books by George S. Counts or Theodore Brameld, or articles which Joseph Junell has published in the *Phi Delta Kappan* magazine in recent years. Also see *Teaching Public Issues in the High School* by Oliver and Shaver (Boston: Houghton Mifflin, 1966) and Shaver's excellent article in the *Journal of Environmental Education* for Fall 1972.

RESEARCH IN EE

Research in EE might be directed at many questions for which answers are needed. What methods are effective in establishing a sense of wonder in young children, a propensity for responsible action in older children?

Formal research studies in EE and related areas, as they have been conceived heretofore, are not likely to produce a very useful set of answers to such important questions. This is the conclusion of some who have reviewed the research already done in conservation education, in outdoor education, in the newer EE, and, for that matter, in education generally.[17] The reasons given are several, but they can be synthesized as follows: First, it is very difficult to measure validly the impact of an education program upon human learning. Too many influences outside the educational program operate to confound the results. Second, great resources of money and talent have never been available to do such research. These two factors are negatively reciprocal. That is, invalid research does not encourage institutions to pour resources into the research effort, and limited resources tend to preclude valid research. Thus, each research study is usually done by a graduate student, on a once-in-a-lifetime basis. The researcher tests teaching method A against teaching method B, then records the results in a thesis, which is filed away on a shelf in a college library. Methods A and B are not further refined and revised in the classroom. Fortunately, progress in education does not rely completely on the results of such research. One critic points out that it is better to engage in "total curricular development" than to do "real research."[18] In the former process, teaching ideas and instructional materials are developed on an intuitive basis. These are then tried, revised, and tried again by classroom teachers until they have something that seems to work. Curriculum developments in education have more often depended upon this kind of process than upon a direct application of research results.

One piece of research that has attracted favorable comment—even from the critics—is the doctoral dissertation by Robert Roth. He prepared a long list of environmental concepts that students ought to learn. These were subjected to successive stages of refining, with the assistance of experts in environment-related fields. A final list of 111 concepts consisted of those found acceptable by 90 percent of the experts, who represented forty professional fields. Roth suggested that the concepts were more representative of contemporary EE than the conservation concepts found in traditional school programs. The concepts are listed in a report of the study in the *Journal of Environmental Education* (Spring 1970): 65-74.

Anyone wishing to see a summary of formal research in EE through September 1972 should obtain *A Review of Research Related to EE*, by Robert E. Roth and Stanley L. Helgeson, published by the ERIC/SMEAC Center, 400 Lincoln Tower, Ohio State University, Columbus, Ohio, 43210.

PROFESSIONAL READING

Journal of Environmental Education, published quarterly by Dembar Educational Research Services, Inc., Box 1605, Madison, Wisconsin, 53701. An excellent journal with articles aimed at a mixed audience of classroom teachers, park naturalists, journalism professors, and others.

Environmental Education Report, monthly, Environmental Educators, Inc., 1621 Connecticut Avenue N.W., Washington, D.C., 20009. Excellent but, like the preceding journal, for a varied audience. Contains information on newly published instructional materials, and brief items of interest mainly to those wishing to stay attuned to the political fortunes of EE.

A few books provide overviews of the new field of EE, though they differ markedly in approach from each other and from the present volume:

TROOST, CORNELIUS, J., and ALTMAN, HAROLD (eds.). *Environmental Education: A Sourcebook*. New York: John Wiley & Sons, 1972. Collection of articles on ecology and environmental problems by excellent authorities, plus articles on EE theory and practice, and sample lessons from EE programs. The examples are too dominated by science; some examples and articles are weak. Overall a very good book, however.

SCHOENFELD, CLAY (ed.). *Outlines of Environmental Education*. Madison, Wisc. Dembar Educational Research Services (P.O. Box 1605, zip 53701), 1971. A collection of articles from the first two years of *Journal of Environmental Education*.

Some introductory books are devoted to the author's view of what EE should be. Two recommended books are:

TERRY, MARK. *Teaching for Survival*. New York: Ballantine Books, 1971.
McINNIS, NOEL. *You Are an Environment*. Evanston, Ill.: Center for Curriculum Design (P.O. Box 350), 1972.

With the exception of the three books named below, no attempt is made here to list books dealing with our environmental-ecological situation, since libraries and college bookstores contain large collections of them. However, we recommend that you watch for the following names, either as authors, editors, or contributors. Apologies to those omitted.

Marston Bates	René Dubos
Kenneth E. Boulding	Paul R. Ehrlich
Lynton Caldwell	Garrett Hardin
Rachel Carson	Ezra Mishan
LaMont Cole	Eugene P. Odum
Barry Commoner	Howard T. Odum
F. Fraser Darling	Paul B. Sears
Raymond F. Dasmann	Nathaniel B. Zalinsky
William O. Douglas	

In addition to the above generalists, some specialists have contributed to indepth books telling "where we are" with respect to energy, water, minerals, open space, wildlife, and other resources. Among the best of these books, filled with hard facts, concepts, and trends, are:

Commission on Population Growth and the American Future. *Population, Resources, and the Environment*. Washington, D.C.: U.S. Government Printing Office, 1972.
MURDOCH, WILLIAM W. (ed.). *Environment: Resources, Pollution, and Society*. Stamford, Conn.: Sinauer Associates (20 Second Street), 1971.
National Academy of Sciences — National Research Council. *Resources and Man*. San Francisco: W. H. Freeman, 1969.

Conclusion

In these last few paragraphs I am going to slip into occasional use of the first-person singular to express some personal opinions.

In a small book dealing with a large and controversial topic, there is the constant danger of overstatement or omission by the author, of misinterpretation by the reader. Perhaps we run that risk in these final few comments, especially.

I am deeply concerned about the status of EE. Some of the better EE projects around the country are also some of the most insecure financially. Consider that in 1973 only 50 of 1,130 proposals were funded under the terms of the Environmental Education Act. (The workshop described in Chapter 4 represents one of these.) Thus, we have a select group of projects and personnel, each supported for only one year by an agency whose own future is insecure at best. When the funds dry up, the field will be left to those with firmer, long-term positions in universities, government agencies, and other institutions. Some of these individuals have failed as yet to demonstrate much competence regarding the goals, content, and methodology of EE. This unfortunate paradox is certainly one deterrent to unbridled optimism about the future of EE.

In this book, I have tried to restrain my considerable impatience with the trivial and irrelevant courses that all too often pass for EE. I should like to share my library with those who are perpetuating such curriculums. In my files are dozens of references compiled for this book, which could not be included or adequately explained in so brief a space. For instance, there is considerable documentation of industry backlash against the new public concern for the environment. There have been misleading advertising campaigns, brazenly fallacious arguments in favor of "business as usual," false charges that environmentalists have caused plant closures, and personal attacks of various kinds. There are several well-documented instances of persons being mysteriously fired from their jobs after speaking out on behalf of the

96

environment. Whereas the actions of the private sector have often been commendable, some of its responses should be no source of self-pride.

Government agencies, too, have presented us with a mixed bag: my files are replete with the good and the bad, the farsighted and the shortsighted. Some of the federal resource agencies are not powerful; they must sometimes yield to demands that are not in the best interest of the public or of posterity. Some agencies are powerful; their budgets are spent on dams and ditches, which many interpret to be ecologically unsound makework projects.

The environmental voting records of our elected representatives speak for themselves: some are environmentally brilliant, others abysmal.

Implicit in all this is a point the reader must comprehend if he is to be an effective environmental educator or an effective citizen. Today an environmental battle is raging on many fronts. It is a very real battle; in fact, it might better be called a war. At its best, it is a war pitting the honest, selfless, rational, and farsighted against the honest, selfless, rational, and nearsighted. At its worst . . .

Too many Americans are passive bystanders to this war, largely unaware of it, scarcely understanding it. Such astute observers of the American scene as John Gardner, Ralph Nader, and Max Lerner have for years been appealing to these people to become an *un*silent majority, to gain a "sense of mission" (Lerner), a "new kind of patriotism" (Nader), a "common cause" (Gardner). We are not concerned here with the political ideologies or specific policies recommended by these men, but rather with the process that they espouse. They are appealing for a participatory democracy in which a broader segment of the citizenry earn the right to be called just that—*citizens*. The citizen conservation groups to which we have frequently alluded should serve as models to the many in this regard.

Shifting to the world scene, we find that the prospects are perfectly clear. The projection of too many current trends leads inevitably to ugliness, social decay, hunger, and constant warfare over the planet's remaining resources. The only feasible alternative is nothing less than a new Renaissance, a whole new change in world-view among the world's peoples. The magnitude of the change is supermonumental. It will have to be more widespread, more profound, and more sudden than the Renaissance of five centuries ago. To live at one with the earth, on a global basis, will be far and away the greatest challenge ever faced by man.

If he faces it.

And that is what EE is all about.

Notes

INTRODUCTION

1. Alec Campbell and Graham Child, "The Impact of Man on the Environment of Botswana," *Botswana Notes and Records* 3 (1971): 91-110.

2. My notes contain references to some eighteen articles, books, or other materials documenting this statement. The classic work in this area, originally published in 1864, is: George Perkins Marsh, *Man and Nature* (Cambridge, Mass.: Harvard University Press, 1965).

3. *World Energy Supplies, 1961-1970* (New York: United Nations Statistical Office). Cited in "World Energy Use Rises 63% in Decade," *Conservation News* 38, no. 13 (July 1, 1973): 10-11. This and notes 4-14, below, represent but a casual and cursory sample of specific, well-documented environmental problems.

4. *World EQ Index* (Washington: National Wildlife Federation, 1972), p. 9.

5. "Depletion of Natural Resources Must Halt, Commission Warns," *Population Crisis* 9, no. 2 (July-August, 1973): 4.

6. *World EQ Index*, p. 8.

7. Ibid., 5-6.

8. *Ecology: Habits and Habitats* (Columbus: American Education Publications, 1971), p. 45.

9. "Massive 'Accidental' Eagle Kill Laid to Trappers," *Conservation News* 38, no. 13 (July 1, 1973): 2-4.

10. Harry M. Caudill, "Strip Mining: Partnership in Greed," *American Forests* 79, no. 5 (May 1973): 16-19.

11. Letter from René Dubos to environmentalists, on behalf of Natural Resources Defense Council, July 1973.

12. *Economic Priorities Reports* (New York: Council on Economic Priorities). Cited in "Steel Industry Flunks CEP Exam," *Conservation News* 38, no. 13 (July 1, 1973): 13.

13. *The U.S. Public Considers Its Environment* (Washington: National Wildlife Federation, 1969). The final report of a study commissioned by NWF and performed by the Gallup Organization. Similarly, a 1969 survey by the National Rural Electric Cooperative Association revealed that 82 percent of the fourteen hundred persons interviewed — two-thirds of them urban — would

rather live in small towns or other rural areas *(Portland Oregonian*, March 2, 1969, p. 21).

14. *1973 EQ Index* (Washington: National Wildlife Federation, 1973).

15. Sen. Abraham A. Ribicoff, "Needed: New Directions for Rural America," *Reader's Digest* 93: no. 557 (September 1968): 107-12; Athelstan Spilhaus, "The Experimental City," *Science* 159, no. 3816 (February 16, 1968): 710-15.

16. Edward Goldsmith et al., *Blueprint for Survival* (Boston: Houghton Mifflin, 1972).

CHAPTER 1

1. My notes contain references to nineteen articles, books, or other materials which state this opinion.

2. Noel McInnis, *You Are an Environment* (Evanston, Ill.: Center for Curriculum Design, 1972), pp. 10-13.

3. R. Thomas Tanner, "Operating Manual for Rachel Carson High," Vol. 1 of 8, *Final Report, Project No. 1-0839, Grant No. OEG-0-71-4623.* (Corvallis, Oreg.: School District 509J, 1972), p. 2.

4. George E. Arnstein, "What *Is* Environmental Education?" *Journal of Environmental Education* 3, no. 1 (Fall 1971): 7-9.

5. Paul Studebaker, "The Justification for Environmental Education," *Journal of Environmental Education* 4, no. 4 (Summer 1973): 48.

6. Clay Schoenfeld, "After the Teach-Ins. . . . What?" *Journal of Environmental Education* 2, no. 1 (Fall 1970): 5.

7. Detailed reports of a number of ROS and other outdoor programs can be obtained from the ERIC/SMEAC Center, 400 Lincoln Tower, Ohio State University, Columbus, Ohio, 43210. In hardcopy or microfiche.

8. Judy Scott, "You Taught Me Social Studies. Now I'm Going to Teach You How to Ice Skate," *Sensorsheet* (Environmental Studies Project and Earth Science Teacher Preparation Project) (Spring 1972): 1.

9. Stanley L. Helgeson et al., *A Review of Environmental Education for Elementary and Secondary School Teachers* (Columbus: Ohio State University, 1971), p. 9.

10. Martha T. Henderson, *Environmental Education* (Boulder, Colo.: Social Science Education Consortium, n.d.), p. iv.

11. *Environmental Education Information Reports: A Directory of Projects and Programs in Environmental Education for Elementary and Secondary Schools* (Columbus: ERIC/SMEAC Center, Ohio State University, 1972), p. iii.

12. Educational Progress Information Exchange, "Assessing Environmental Education Materials," *Journal of Environmental Education* 3, no. 1 (Fall 1971): 42.

13. *Environmental Education Handbook (Public Law 91-516)* (Washington: Office of Environmental Education, U.S. Office of Education, undated draft—1973), p. 3.

14. Elizabeth Beirne, "Bringing Environmental Education to the Bronx," *Journal of Environmental Education* 3, no. 2 (Winter 1971): 3.

15. Willis L. Hobart, "What's Wrong with Conservation Education?" *Journal of Environmental Education* 3, no. 4 (Summer 1972): 25.

16. R. Thomas Tanner, "Environmental Pseudo-Holism," *Education Division News* 1, no. 4 (August 1972): 1.

17. Scott, "You Taught Me Social Studies," p. 1.

18. *The Web* 1, no. 1. It should be noted that Open Space, Inc., the organization producing this periodical also engages in activities very appropriate to EE.

19. Eugene M. Ezersky, "Priorities of Environmental Concern," *Journal of Environmental Education* 3, no. 4 (Summer 1972): 11.

20. *Environmental Education Handbook (Public Law 91-516)*, p. 9.

21. Clay Schoenfeld, "George Lowe, Take a Bow," *Journal of Environmental Education* 4, no. 4 (Summer 1973): 65.

22. Clay Schoenfeld, "On Environmental Studies," *Journal of Environmental Education* 2, no. 2 (Winter 1970): 49.

23. Paul A. Yambert and Jerry Gafney, "Environmental Education: A Personal Definition" (Unpublished paper, Southern Illinois University, 1972).

24. R. Thomas Tanner, "Position Paper on Environmental Education" (Unpublished paper, Oregon State University, 1972).

25. Schoenfeld, "George Lowe, Take a Bow," p. 65.

26. *Environmental Education Handbook (Public Law 91-516)*, pp. 3-9.

27. McInnis, *You Are an Environment*, p. 72.

28. Ibid., 27.

29. Fred W. Fox, "Forces Influencing Education: Present and Future," in *Design for Progress in Science Education*, ed. David P. Butts (Austin: Science Education Center, University of Texas, 1970); Paul DeHart Hurd, "The Scientific Enterprise and the Educated Citizen: An Unfinished Task" (Paper presented at a meeting of the Kansas City [Missouri] Science Teachers Association, November 17, 1967).

30. Frank M. Rice, *English and Its Teaching* (Lincoln, Nebr.: Professional Educators Publications, 1972), pp. 25, 30; Randall C. Anderson, *Current Trends in Secondary School Social Studies* (Lincoln, Nebr.: Professional Educators Publications, 1972), pp. 59-82.

31. *Environmental Education Handbook (Public Law 91-516)*, p. 6.

32. Alan Gussow, *A Sense of Place: The Artist and the American Land* (San Francisco: Friends of the Earth, 1971), pp. 27-33.

33. Edith Cobb, "The Ecology of Imagination in Childhood" and Grady Clay, "Remembered Landscapes," both in *The Subversive Science: Essays toward an Ecology of Man*, ed. Paul Shepard and Daniel McKinley (Boston: Houghton Mifflin, 1969), pp. 122-32 and 133-39.

34. Les Line, "Why I Became a 'Preservationist,' " *Smithsonian* 4, no. 4 (July 1973): 72-74.

35. It is worth noting, incidentally, that the authors of a book reviewing more than eighty-five research studies in EE state that none of the studies considered EE on other than a local, regional, or national basis. Robert E. Roth and Stanley L. Helgeson, *A Review of Research Related to Environmental Education* (Columbus, Ohio, 43221: ERIC/SMEAC Center, 400 Lincoln Tower, 1972), p. 43.

36. John Dewey, *Experience and Education* (New York: Macmillan, 1938). A famous satire deals with the same—and other—topics: Harold Benjamin [J. Abner Peddiwell], *The Saber-Tooth Curriculum* (New York: McGraw-Hill, 1939). The reader will find that both of these books are still quite relevant today; the latter is always a favorite of education students.

CHAPTER 2

1. *Ekistics* (Sacramento: California State Department of Education, draft form), cited in *"Ekistics—A* Preview" (book review), *Journal of Environmental Education* 3, no. 4 (Summer 1972): 17.

2. Dennis J. Clark, "Toward Community Control," *Journal of Environmental Education* 4, no. 2 (Winter 1972): 20-21.

3. Eugene M. Ezersky, "Priorities of Environmental Concern," *Journal of Environmental Education* 3, no. 4 (Summer 1972): 11-12.

4. Barbara J. Reid, "Whither Urban Environmental Education?" *Journal of Environmental Education* 2, no. 1 (Fall 1970): 28-29.

5. *Environmental Education/Facility Resources* (New York: Educational Facilities Laboratories, 1972), p. 25.

6. Elizabeth Beirne, "Bringing Environmental Education to the Bronx," *Journal of Environmental Education* 3, no. 2 (Winter 1971): 3-4.

7. Mary Maxine Boyd, "Taking the Parks to People," *Journal of Environmental Education* 4, no. 2 (Winter 1972): 1-2.

8. Letter from Elvis J. Stahr, Society President, to members of the National Audubon Society, February 10, 1972.

9. Alice Dennis, "Conservationists Turn On for Children of the Concrete," *National Parks and Conservation Magazine* (June 1970). Reprinted in *Environmental Education: A Sourcebook,* ed. Cornelius J. Troost and Harold Altman (New York: John Wiley & Sons, 1972), pp. 374-78.

10. Clay Schoenfeld, "Learning the Great Lesson," *Journal of Environmental Education* 1, no. 4 (Summer 1970): 153.

11. René Dubos, *Smithsonian,* issue unknown.

12. Letter from Elvis J. Stahr, February 10, 1972.

13. Beverly H. Southern, "Vitalizing Natural Resources Education," *Journal of Environmental Education* 1, no. 1 (Fall 1969): 29.

14. *A Place to Live: Teacher's Manual* (New York: National Audubon Society, 1970), p. 3.

15. Cornelius J. Troost and Harold Altman, eds., *Environmental Education: A Sourcebook* (New York: John Wiley & Sons, 1972).

16. Matthew J. Brennan, remarks at an EE conference, Portland, Oregon, June 1969.

17. Alan M. Voelker, "Supplementary Readers in Environmental Education" (Paper presented at the Annual Convention of the Wisconsin Education Association, Milwaukee, November 5, 1970), p. 3; Sheryl Schoenfeld, "Environmental Ecological Education: Resources for Elementary and Secondary Schools" (book review), *Journal of Environmental Education* 3, no. 3 (Spring 1972): 43.

18. *A Place To Live: Teacher's Manual,* p. 3.

19. "The Great Dismal Swamp," *Nature Conservancy News* 23, no. 2 (Spring 1973): 6-13.

20. In another book in the Professional Education Series, Dr. Frank M. Rice points out that the teaching of literature in recent years has been somewhat influenced by a theory which holds that younger children should study comedy and romance; older ones, irony and tragedy. The parallel to the sequence suggested here is interesting.

21. *ESsense* (Boulder, Colo.: Environmental Studies Project, 1970).

22. Robert E. Roth, "The Environment and Man," *Journal of Environmental Education* 3, no. 3 (Spring 1972): 45.

23. John C. Hendee, "No, to Attitudes to Evaluate Environmental Education," *Journal of Environmental Education* 3, no. 3 (Spring 1972): 65.

24. Southern, "Vitalizing National Resources Education," p. 29.

25. Roger Tory Peterson, "Birds Are Environmental Litmus Paper" (Address delivered at the Annual Audubon Dinner, National Audubon Society, New York, November 1971). Reprinted in *Education Division News* 1, no. 1 (February 1972): 9-10.

26. Ben D. Mahaffey, "A Day With Freeman Tilden," *Journal of Environmental Education* 2, no. 4 (Summer 1971): 31.

27. Clay Schoenfeld, "After the Teach-Ins. . . . What?" *Journal of Environmental Education* 2, no. 1 (Fall 1970): 6.

28. Walter Herrscher, "Changing Concepts in American Nature Writing," *Journal of Environmental Education* 4, no. 1 (Fall 1972): 39.

29. Sheryl Schoenfeld (book review), "Environmental Ecological Education."

30. Clay Schoenfeld, "What's New About Environmental Education?" *Journal of Environmental Education* 1, no. 1 (Fall 1969): 1-4.

31. Clay Schoenfeld, "After the Teach-Ins. . . . What?" p. 4.

32. For instance, a review highly critical of a teacher's guide from one federal agency appears in *Journal of Environmental Education* (Fall 1971): 15.

CHAPTER 4

1. *Living River—Grand Canyon.* Sierra Club films are available from AS/CCM Films, 866 Third Avenue, New York, N.Y. 10022. West of the Rockies they are available also from a voluntary citizens' group, the Conservation Film Center, 3215 NE 103rd Street, Seattle, Wash., 98125 or 21315 NE Sahalee Drive, Redmond, Wash., 98052. Free loan.

2. John McPhee, *Encounters with the Archdruid* (New York: Farrar, Straus & Giroux, 1971), pp. 164-65; Grant McConnell, "Prologue: Environment and the Quality of Political Life," in *Congress and the Environment,* ed. Richard A. Cooley and Geoffrey Wandesforde-Smith (Seattle: University of Washington Press, 1970), pp. 3-15.

3. "Opposition" literature includes the following: "Stemming the Flood at Lake Powell," *Sierra Club Bulletin* 58, no. 4 (April 1973): 21; "Rainbow

Not Saved," *Environmental Action* 4, no. 24 (April 28, 1973): 2; George Alderson, "Rainbow Bridge Is Being Drowned, Being Drowned. . . .," *Environmental Action* 5, no. 3 (June 23, 1973): 3-5; "New Predictions of Danger to Rainbow Bridge: Arch Might Crash in 5 to 25 years," *Not Man Apart* 3, no. 7 (July 1973): 5.

On May 14, 1973, we wrote to the Bureau of Reclamation as follows:

Films and publications from such groups as the Sierra Club and Friends of the Earth have taken a position of opposition to, first, the construction of Glen Canyon Dam and, second, the complete filling of Lake Powell. As a teacher wishing his students to be exposed to *all* sides of issues, I would appreciate any information or publications you may have to represent your position regarding these specific issues. Thank you.

Unfortunately, the materials received in response were all promotional brochures, not directed to this issue at all. Write: U.S. Department of the Interior, Bureau of Reclamation, Engineering and Research Center, Building 67, Denver Federal Center, Denver, Colo., 80225.

4. McPhee, *Encounters with the Archdruid*, pp. 151-245.

5. Chapter 12, "Down the River," in Abbey, *Desert Solitaire* (New York: McGraw-Hill, 1968).

6. In the sequence used, these are: *Operation Glen Canyon*, Bureau of Reclamation, Film Management Center, Building 67, Denver Federal Center, Denver, Colo., 80225; *Glen Canyon*, see note 1 above for addresses; *Lake Powell—Jewel of the Colorado*, Bureau of Reclamation, address above. All available on free loan.

7. *The River* is available from many university film libraries.

8. Spenser W. Havlick, "A Glimpse and Analysis of Environmental Education Opportunities in American Higher Education," *Journal of Environmental Education* 1, no. 1 (Fall 1969): 24.

9. John H. Trent, "Are Teacher Education Colleges Increasing Their Environmental Education Involvement?" (Paper presented at the Area Convention of the National Science Teachers Association, San Diego, December 2, 1972). Also, at the time of this writing the Wisconsin Environmental Education Council (610 Langdon Street, Madison, Wisc., 53706) was completing a new survey on EE teacher-education programs in 1973.

10. John H. Trent, "Status of Environmental Education as Perceived by State Departments of Education" (Unpublished paper, University of Nevada —Reno, 1972).

11. "Classes in the Open Air," *Journal of Environmental Education* 3, no. 2 (Winter 1971): 56. Reprinted from *Pennsylvania Education* (November-December 1970).

12. Advisory Council on Environmental Education, "Second Annual Report" (Washington: U.S. Office of Education, 1973), pp. 1-6.

13. John C. Hendee, "No, to Attitudes to Evaluate Environmental Education," *Journal of Environmental Education* 3, no. 3 (Spring 1972): 65.

104 NOTES

14. R. Thomas Tanner, "Freedom and a Varied Environment," *Science Teacher* 36, no. 4 (April 1969): 32-34.

15. Association for Supervision and Curriculum Development of the National Education Association, *Large Was Our Bounty: Natural Resources and the Schools* (Washington: National Education Association, 1948), p. 7.

16. Some reversals of these trends in recent months will, if continued, have interesting effects on the EE climate. Escalating inflation and shortages of fuel and other materials may lead to a greater raid on resources, and to an "ecology-be-damned attitude," which in the long run can only be self-defeating.

17. Hendee, "No, to Attitudes to Evaluate Environmental Education," p. 65; Dana L. Abell, "The Journal of Environmental Education," *Journal of Environmental Education* 2, no. 4 (Summer 1971): 2. Reprinted from *Bio-Science* (September 15, 1970).

18. Abell, "Journal of Environmental Education," p. 2.

Selected Bibliography

The following list includes recommended readings for which bibliographic information is not given elsewhere in this book.

AMIDEI, ROSEMARY E.; FREDERICK, CHARLES L.; and YAGER, ROBERT (eds.). *Environment: The Human Impact*. Washington: National Science Teachers Association, 1973. Articles selected from past issues of the *Science Teacher*. Arranged into four sections: personal perspectives on the nature of the problem; background on specific problems; descriptions of school programs; directions for specific teaching techniques.

BODSWORTH, FRED. *Last of the Curlews*. New York: Dodd, Mead, 1954. A classic, heart-rending novel of the wild, with an EE message.

BRANSON, BRANLEY A. "Outline: A Program of Eco-Environmental Education." *Journal of Environmental Education* 4, no. 2 (Winter, 1972): 3-18. A listing of tough-minded concepts, to complement those concentrated in three other works: the books by Hawkins and the National Association for EE, below, and the research article by Roth, discussed in Chapter 4.

CARSON, RACHEL. *The Sense of Wonder*. New York: Harper & Row, 1956. How to help small children gain a sense of wonder at the world of nature.

GARY, ROMAIN. *The Roots of Heaven*. New York: Simon & Schuster, 1958. Novel about a small army of idealists who wage war against elephant hunters in West Africa. A real person—the Jesuit philosopher Teilhard de Chardin—plays an interesting role. This won the Prix Goncourt, France's top literary prize.

HAWKINS, MARY E. (ed.). *Vital Views of the Environment*. Washington: National Science Teachers Association, 1970. A concentration of concepts by Dasmann, Dubos, Ehrlich, Hardin, and others.

HICKEL, WALTER J. *Who Owns America?* Englewood Cliffs, N.J.: Prentice-Hall, 1971. During the decade of the 1960s, America was blessed with two fine Secretaries of the Interior: Udall and Hickel. Udall's book (see below) gave us historical perspective and contributed to the new popular awareness; Hickel's brings us rudely up to date on contemporary politico-economic realities.

LEOPOLD, ALDO. *A Sand County Almanac*. New York: Oxford University Press, 1949. A classic statement of the joy and beauty found in a life-style

· that is compatible with the earth. The term *land ethic* comes to us largely from this book.

Man and Environment for Secondary Schools. Miami, Fla.: National Association for Environmental Education, 1973. A comprehensive and interdisciplinary set of concepts and student objectives, by a national panel of high school teachers and university consultants, all selected for their EE experience and expertise.

MEADOWS, DONELLA, et al. *The Limits to Growth.* New York: Universe Books, 1972. Computer models of alternative futures for the planet; written nontechnically. The authors of *Blueprint for Survival* acknowledge a considerable debt to this controversial, widely discussed book.

SCHEFFER, VICTOR B. *The Year of the Whale.* New York: Charles Scribner's Sons, 1969. Another highly acclaimed novel of the wild with an EE message. Written by a biologist with the U.S. Fish and Wildlife Service, it has already been declared a classic by many.

THOREAU, HENRY DAVID. *The Portable Thoreau.* New York: Viking Press, 1947. After a century and a quarter, the transcendentalist sage is as meaningful as ever — if not more so. Contains *Walden, A Week on the Concord and Merrimack Rivers,* "Civil Disobedience," and selected essays, poems, and letters.

UDALL, STEWART L. *The Quiet Crisis.* New York: Holt, Rinehart & Winston, 1963. The American land and man's treatment of it, from the Indians and the mountain men to the present. The cast includes not only the despoilers, but mainly those who have shown a better way: Jefferson, Thoreau, Marsh, Powell, Pinchot, Muir, Olmsted, and the Roosevelts. See comments on the book by Hickel, above.